Leadership Strategies for Meeting New Challenges

Alan B. Knox, *Editor*

NEW DIRECTIONS FOR CONTINUING EDUCATION
ALAN B. KNOX, *Editor-in-Chief*

Number 13, March 1982

Paperback sourcebooks in
The Jossey-Bass Higher Education Series

Jossey-Bass Inc., Publishers
San Francisco • Washington • London

Leadership Strategies for Meeting New Challenges
Number 13, March 1982
    Alan B. Knox, *Editor*

New Directions for Continuing Education Series
Alan B. Knox, *Editor-in-Chief*

Copyright © 1982 by Jossey-Bass Inc., Publishers
                and
              Jossey-Bass Limited

Copyright under International, Pan American, and Universal Copyright Conventions. All rights reserved. No part of this issue may be reproduced in any form—except for brief quotation (not to exceed 500 words) in a review or professional work—without permission in writing from the publishers.

New Directions for Continuing Education (publication number USPS 493-930) quarterly by Jossey-Bass Inc., Publishers. Second-class postage rates paid at San Francisco, California, and at additional mailing offices.

Correspondence:
Subscriptions, single-issue orders, change of address notices, undelivered copies, and other correspondence should be sent to *New Directions* Subscriptions, Jossey-Bass Inc., Publishers, 433 California Street, San Francisco, California 94104.

Editorial correspondence should be sent to the Editor-in-Chief, Alan B. Knox, Teacher Education Building, Room 264, University of Wisconsin, 225 North Mills Street, Madison, Wisconsin 53706.

Library of Congress Catalogue Card Number LC 81-48474
International Standard Serial Number ISSN 0195-2242
International Standard Book Number ISBN 87589-887-4

Cover art by Willi Baum
Manufactured in the United States of America

Ordering Information

The paperback sourcebooks listed below are published quarterly and can be ordered either by subscription or as single copies.

Subscriptions cost $35.00 per year for institutions, agencies, and libraries. Individuals can subscribe at the special rate of $21.00 per year *if payment is by personal check.* (Note that the full rate of $35.00 applies if payment is by institutional check, even if the subscription is designated for an individual.) Standing orders are accepted.

Single copies are available at $7.95 when payment accompanies order, and *all single-copy orders under $25.00 must include payment.* (California, Washington, D.C., New Jersey, and New York residents please include appropriate sales tax.) For billed orders, cost per copy is $7.95 plus postage and handling. (Prices subject to change without notice.)

To ensure correct and prompt delivery, all orders must give either the *name of an individual* or an *official purchase order number.* Please submit your order as follows:

Subscriptions: specify series and subscription year.
Single Copies: specify sourcebook code and issue number (such as, CE8).

Mail orders for United States and Possessions, Latin America, Canada, Japan, Australia, and New Zealand to:
    Jossey-Bass Inc., Publishers
    433 California Street
    San Francisco, California 94104

Mail orders for all other parts of the world to:
    Jossey-Bass Limited
    28 Banner Street
    London EC1Y 8QE

New Directions for Continuing Education Series
Alan B. Knox, *Editor-in-Chief*

CE1 *Enhancing Proficiencies of Continuing Educators,* Alan B. Knox
CE2 *Programming for Adults Facing Mid-Life Change,* Alan B. Knox
CE3 *Assessing the Impact of Continuing Education,* Alan B. Knox
CE4 *Attracting Able Instructors of Adults,* M. Alan Brown, Harlan G. Copeland
CE5 *Providing Continuing Education by Media and Technology,* Martin N. Chamberlain
CE6 *Teaching Adults Effectively,* Alan B. Knox
CE7 *Assessing Educational Needs of Adults,* Floyd C. Pennington
CE8 *Reaching Hard-to-Reach Adults,* Gordon G. Darkenwald, Gordon A. Larson
CE9 *Strengthening Internal Support for Continuing Education,* James C. Votruba
CE10 *Advising and Counseling Adult Learners,* Frank R. DiSilvestro
CE11 *Continuing Education for Community Leadership,* Harold W. Stubblefield
CE12 *Attracting External Funds for Continuing Education,* John Buskey

Contents

Editor's Notes 1
Alan B. Knox

Chapter 1. Decision Making 3
New challenges can spur administrators to reexamine personal and situational aspects of decision making.

Chapter 2. Priority Setting 11
Strategies for priority setting accommodate competing goals and expectations of policy makers, administrators, resource persons, and participants.

Chapter 3. Resources 19
Decision making strategies regarding financial and other resources also include attention to purposes, context, and program development.

Chapter 4. Marketing 37
Effective strategies to encourage adult learners to participate include attention to the entire marketing mix.

Chapter 5. Coordinating Programs 53
Program administrators should make valuable contributions to planning committees and emphasize strategic factors that make a difference.

Chapter 6. Staffing 67
Multiple incentives to attract able resource persons and focused orientation activities can contribute to supervisory effectiveness.

Chapter 7. External Relations 85
Pushy diplomacy characterizes a strategy to deal with decentralized power and competing expectations in the parent organization and the service area.

Chapter 8. Discrepancy Analysis 103
Discrepancies between current and desired practice can be vehicles for professional growth.

Index 111

Editor's Notes

Administrators of educational programs for adults in all settings confront many challenges. Some of the basic problems and opportunities endure (such as attracting hard-to-reach adults, obtaining resources, and benefiting from outstanding resource persons), although the specifics may change. Procedures for dealing with long-standing challenges tend to become routine.

Some challenges to continuing education are new (such as dealing with the inflationary cost/price squeeze, with the increased centrality of continuing education, and with competitive relations among an increasing number of providers). Attention to leadership strategies for meeting new challenges is doubly important. More effective decision-making strategies can help meet emerging challenges and some of them may also be useful in responding to long-standing problems and opportunities.

This volume of *New Directions for Continuing Education* suggests some issues for which new insights about leadership strategies seem helpful, and for each issue explores pertinent decision-making concepts and procedures. It also shows how administrators in various settings have (or might) use such concepts to enrich their decision making. Finally, further readings are identified.

Chapter One suggests how personal and situational aspects of decision making can contribute to effective leadership strategies. The next six chapters explore six general types of decisions; presenting examples from continuing education practice and generalizations from research and writing relevant to decision making and leadership. Most of the examples are anonymous accounts provided by administrators in various types of provider agencies. Although hardly representative, they do reflect the strategies of able practitioners who were willing to discuss what they did and why. The broad areas of decision making covered by these six chapters are priority setting, resource acquisition and allocation, marketing, coordinating programs, staffing, and external relations. The chapter on coordinating programs deals with decision making by program administrators and not detailed decisions by teachers of adults.

In practice, strategies to deal with the most important issues tend to cut across a number of these areas of decision making because they are interrelated. For example, priorities should, resources do, and evaluation can influence other decisions. The concluding chapter suggests ways in which continuing education administrators can compare their practices with the concepts and procedures presented in this volume and in the readings listed in the bibliography as a vehicle for their professional development. The most important theme of this volume is that creating more explicit decision-making strategies can contribute to sounder decisions for the agency and enhanced proficiency for those associated with the decision-making process.

It is especially important for practitioners to reflect on leadership strategies because making administrative decisions is a very personal process. The best decision in a specific instance depends on influence related to setting, procedures, and beliefs. This sourcebook does not present the best decisions for the selected issues. Instead, it illustrates a general approach to leadership strategies that focuses attention on five aspects of decision making: conceptual (theories of organization and administration), technical (specialized procedures and information related to each decision), organizational (bureaucratic and political dynamics that affect both decision making and implementation), (human interpersonal relationships), and belief (values, goals, and expectations). The information about the selected decision-making issues should be familiar to most readers, but it provides a vehicle to show how attention to these five aspects can be combined in effective leadership strategies. This sourcebook is designed to encourage continuing education administrators to reflect on their current approach to decision making and to recognize concepts and practices they could use to enrich the process.

Alan B. Knox
Editor

Alan B. Knox is professor of continuing education in the School of Education, University of Wisconsin–Madison. An author of more than eighty publications, he has been an administrator of continuing education at Syracuse University and the University of Illinois at Urbana–Champaign (where he also taught), and was a professor at the University of Nebraska at Lincoln and at Teachers College, Columbia University.

Effective leadership strategies consist of decision-making procedures that take personal expertise and values as well as situational expectations and resources into account, to meet new challenges.

Decision Making

Ernest Trueblood faced a tough decision. Along with teaching in the business department of Franklin Community College with its large and partially separate continuing education division, he served as coordinator of about fifty business courses and workshops through the division. More than half his instructors were from the community and taught at the college part time. Trueblood needed to decide whether or not to appoint Justinian Eagle, a local attorney with no previous connection with the college, to teach an advanced evening credit course on business law. Eagle was also a bank vice-president and had taught a course in business law at the state university law school.

The teacher of the business law course in recent years had been a young faculty member by the name of Casper Wilton. Business law was not a major area of background or interest for Wilton, but there was no one else in the business department who was more prepared and interested, so he agreed to teach it as a favor to the department chairman who had recruited Wilton because of his growing scholarly reputation. Wilton was currently working on his doctorate in economics, and he was interested in teaching the business law course on an overload basis for extra pay.

In the classroom, Wilton tended to be hesitant and somewhat disorganized. He had little practical business experience. His one teaching experience in the continuing education division was not very successful, and there was a 60 percent dropout rate for the adult students in the course. When Trueblood first approached the chairman about offering the business law course through the division and having Eagle teach it, the chairman countered that it was a good idea to offer the couse, but that, if it was offered, Wilton should teach it. In part because he reported to the chairman for the teaching half of his assignment, Trueblood hesitated to take issue with his seemingly firm position during their first encounter on the topic.

Trueblood subsequently visited informally about the matter with the director of the continuing education division. He stressed to the director the backlog of interest and requests from the community for a business law course and the fact that many of the potential class members were business people of some influence, especially in relation to authorizing tuition reimbursement arrangements for employees who enrolled in the division. The director indicated that in the past, the decision on staffing credit courses had been a mutual one and that there was little that could be done if the chairman insisted on Wilton instead of Eagle—other than not offering the course (at least on a credit basis). The director, however, did indicate that he was sympathetic to Trueblood's views on the matter.

After considering several alternatives, Trueblood decided to use available funds for a business education needs assessment project that would entail analyzing economic data and contacting local businesses. He discussed this with Wilton, including the possibility of his conducting the study for the division. The division director agreed that Wilton could be paid as much for doing so as for teaching the business law course, and that each assignment would take about the same amount of time. When Trueblood next discussed the alternatives with Wilton, he mentioned the publication possibilities, and Wilton expressed his preference for conducting the project. Both the chairman and the director agreed and Trueblood hired Eagle to teach the course.

This fictional case, based on findings from Daigneault's (1963) study, addresses a modest problem, but it illustrates several important features of decision making by continuing education program administrators. Half-time and full-time administrators in continuing education agencies and in parent organizations are very involved in decisions about continuing education programs. Most participants and resource persons are part-time and although influential in decisions involving their own courses and workshops, are little involved in overall agency planning. Most importantly, it shows how an administrator used a decision-making strategy to solve a problem.

The Administrator's Role

Decision making is a major administrative task in any setting. Administration includes attention to both stability and change, and so does decision making (Darkenwald, 1977). Many decisions pertain to achieving and maintaining agency stability and equilibrium so that resources are available for adult learners and teachers to pursue growth and change. Because most continuing education agencies lack many ingredients that contribute to stability (such as policies, dependable financing, full-time staff, and their own facilities), the temporary arrangements that administrators negotiate may be the cement that holds the agency together. Other decisions pertain to solving problems that emerge, and still others relate to planning in order to achieve desirable changes and avoid undesirable ones.

Continuing education occurs in many settings. Some agencies that provide it are parts of educational institutions such as schools, colleges, or universities. Even more of continuing education is provided by agencies that are parts of many other types of organizations such as employers, unions, associations, religious institutions, libraries, museums, penal institutions, hospitals, and community agencies. In each of these settings, there are some issues that are especially important. These issues may relate to setting priorities, managing resources, marketing, developing programs, staffing, external relations, or other aspects of agency functioning. Effective decision-making strategies reflect the specifics of the settings and issues with which they deal. This volume includes generalizations and examples related to the various settings and issues that continuing education administrators confront.

Some insights about decision making are transferrable from one issue or setting to another. One such insight is that administrators can benefit from the experience of others regarding the process of decision making. Reading about or discussing strategies used by other administrators, or reviewing highlights from writings on decision making can help administrators improve their decision-making strategies and make them more explicit. Having a rationale for one's approach to decision making can be especially helpful when dealing with changing realities and new problems for which traditional solutions seem inadequate (Knox, 1975).

Being explicit about decision making also helps an administrator utilize concepts and approaches that have widespread applicability in many continuing education settings and to be responsive to the distinctive features of each situation. For example, the importance of adult learning and teaching and of program development procedures makes concepts about adult development especially relevant to many administrative decisions about continuing education. Also, the power-poor position of most continuing education administrators (who must rely heavily on persuasion and winning cooperation) makes it difficult to use some concepts that assume an executive model for decision making more appropriate for the chief executive officer of a large organization such as a university, business, hospital, or school system.

Many basics of administrative decision making are reflected in even a simple example such as deciding how to respond to a letter of inquiry about program offerings. Many alternatives exist, only some of which may be considered by an administrator. In this instance the administrator may write a note on the letter and return it, ask the secretary to send one of two form letters (one accompanying a catalogue and encouraging registration, or one indicating that the agency does not have relevant offerings and suggesting other providers that do), compose a letter responding to specific questions asked, have someone in the agency draft a response, or prepare a letter and arrange for special treatment (such as a follow-up call, adding the person's name to the agency mailing list, or an invitation to join the advisory committee). Even not replying is a decision, in that the writer of the letter is ignored. Not to make a decision is to allow circumstances to decide. In some instances, this course can be desirable.

Decision making, then, is choosing one or a combination of alternatives, some of which may not be immediately recognized. The alternatives to be considered depend in part on how the decider(s) may perceive the problem or the question calling for a decision and how important and well defined it is. In response to a letter of inquiry, a director with well-defined offerings and a clear idea of the institution's clientele may respond routinely, whereas a director trying to clarify target markets may see responding to the letter as part of an important and uncertain marketing task. The alternative that is eventually selected depends on what is valued by those making the decision, including both the criteria for selecting the preferred solution and the importance of the decision (and thus how much time and effort to invest in deciding). The director making a routine response is likely to select the least expensive alternative that will encourage a registration, whereas the director attempting to use inquiries to clarify target markets may invest more money in a response that may open up a new clientele and program area.

Related considerations in decision making include deciding who on the agency staff is affected and thus should help decide how to respond, assessing how much experience and data are available to predict the likely outcomes for each alternative, using a creative process for generating alternatives, and ascertaining that major influences and effects of alternatives are recognized and dealt with. The process of choosing also includes taking both precedent and policy into account. Another consideration is using a decision-making process that also encourages implementation.

In addition to the typical ingredients of the process of decision making, the characteristics of decision makers influence both the process and the outcome. Many administrators think of decision making as their domain and of the deciding process as implicit in the ways they make choices and solve problems. Thus the decisions they consider and the procedures they use reflect the types of problems, opportunities, and choices they perceive and value (Pepper, 1958). As a result, their decision making reflects such personal characteristics as how decisively they make difficult choices, how willing they are to take risks, and how much complexity they are able to deal with. Their decision making also reflects how intuitive their approach is—in contrast with being able to make the process explicit so that others can easily take part—as well as their concern for including other people in the process.

For inexperienced administrators, decision making tends to be a personal process, largely influenced by their personalities, experiences, and perceptions of local circumstances. Effective administrators realize that decision making should be more explicit and public because it is a means of working with and through other people to serve the two main functions of leadership in any setting: achieving agreement on important objectives and encouraging people to contribute to the achievement of those objectives. Two advantages of explicit decision making are that it encourages other people to contribute to both making and implementing sounder decisions, and that the process can be enriched by increased familiarity with information about decision-making concepts and procedures.

Program Development and Clientele

Many major decisions relate to program development and assistance to adult learners, even indirectly. Alternative choices about new programs, financial support, staff selection, and external collaboration are weighed in part on their contribution to program development. Program development alternatives are considered in part in relation to achieving specific objectives for a specific clientele. Thus decision making entails chains of connected decisions in which alternatives considered for a decision are influenced by previous choices and the decision that is made influences subsequent choices. Furthermore, different combinations of people can be involved in each decision in the chain (Collins and Guetzkow, 1964). Effective administrators anticipate probable decisions and prepare for them. Failure to do so can lead to breakdowns in decision making such as the widespread error of trying to start on too large a scale.

This is illustrated by the efforts of a continuing higher education division to start a liberal studies external degree program for adults. The idea was attractive to both the assistant director of the continuing education division and the assistant dean of liberal arts. They both read about such programs elsewhere, attended a meeting of external degree administrators, and visited several similar institutions with exemplary programs. They informally discussed some preliminary ideas about creating an external degree with key faculty members and administrators, and there was agreement about its desirability and its multiple benefits to the college, the division, and the institution generally.

A needs assessment was conducted to estimate the size, characteristics, and interests of the clientele. A faculty committee reviewed a background document based on the review of other programs and the needs assessment and met with a consultant from one of the excellent programs offered elsewhere. The committee recommended that planning proceed. This recommendation was endorsed by key administrators, more detailed market research was done, and a faculty committee prepared a proposal that consisted mainly of a rationale for why a new external degree was desirable and what its structure would be. Both the assistant director of continuing education and the faculty committee agreed that an entire external degree program should be established at the outset so that adults who enrolled in their first course would be assured that all of the remaining parts of the degree program were scheduled and would follow.

So far, so good. The proposal was approved and all concerned agreed that it was desirable. Then, as the process shifted from planning to implementation, the consensus began to fall apart. The faculty member who had chaired the faculty committee and who was slated to be project director withdrew. Mildly expressed concerns about resources snowballed and became impediments to progress. When no mutually satisfactory project director was forthcoming, the proposal had to be scrapped. In retrospect, the assistant director concluded that a sounder strategy would have been to involve committed faculty members in a pilot effort. This would have reduced resistance due to apprehension about competition for scarce resources, provided tangible examples of how the program would function, and built support within the college to obtain satisfaction with both the process and the results, and in general allowed the program to evolve at a slower pace.

By contrast, the newly appointed director of a large but stagnant public school adult education program took an evolutionary approach to decision making. He had been a part-time teacher of vocational adult education for many years before his early retirement from business. During his early months as director, while the long-time assistant director supervised the existing program, the director talked with many teachers and administrators, reviewed agency records and reports, and talked with others in the service area. Not only was the program he inherited sluggish, but other local providers were not. He would have to compete in a turbulent environment just as he had in business. He analyzed each aspect of his agency by describing current characteristics and trends, desirable characteristics, and how the agency might be improved. The director informally discussed major conclusions with a few key people and began to establish networks of allies who were interested in strengthening the adult and continuing education program. New projects were viewed both as serving adult learners and as building a positive image and needed support for new program directions for the entire agency. Program ideas, talented teachers, and available resources were viewed as targets of opportunity when they fit his general plan. His strategy was to "plant seeds," allow time and resources for progress to occur, and to "nudge" where needed to achieve consensus or maintain momentum.

In summary, administrative decision making is a complex process that is both personal and situational. Although choosing among alternative courses of action seems to be the focus, the process includes attention to the context in which decisions are made and implemented, mastery of technical procedures, interpersonal relations, consideration of both individual and organizational values, and concepts about organization and administration. Some decisions may benefit from PERT charting, in which the network of tasks required to accomplish an objective are diagrammed so that the sequence of branching decisions can be easily scanned and time estimates and prerequisites established. Other decisions entail conflicts of values. In these situations, effective administrators provide the diplomacy to achieve consensus and the courage and perseverance to follow through and achieve the objective with and through others. This volume does not suggest the decisions that should be made or even the best process for making them. Instead, its intent is to encourage continuing education administrators to reflect on their current decision-making strategies and to identify ways to strengthen the process.

The following chapters use basic information about decisions that continuing education administrators typically confront as illustrations of how decision-making strategies can be enriched by using various concepts to guide administrative action. Such concepts reflect both the art and the science of administration as a process of accomplishing results with and through other people. Mastery of such concepts aids recognition of the strategic factors that contribute to success. The following three aspects of decision making each contribute to affect leadership strategies:

1. Belief—the values, goals, and expectations of people associated with the decision-making process.

2. Human—the interpersonal relations that affect the cooperation that is essential for implementation of decisions.

3. Organizational—the bureaucratic and political dynamics that influence the decision-making process and are reflected in bargaining and compromise.

Both general concepts and technical expertise contribute to the process of making and implementing major administrative decisions through attention to all three of these aspects. Implementation entails attention to leadership as well as planning and choosing; attention to belief, human, and organizational aspects contribute to cooperation. This is the rationale for the entire volume, which illustrates the interplay of these aspects of decision making in specific instances and shows how information from other people about relevant concepts and practices can be used to enrich leadership strategies.

New challenges can affect agency priorities, which reflect competing goals and multiple influences. Effective leadership strategies accommodate the competing expectations of policy makers, agency staff, resource persons, and participants.

Priority Setting

Some decisions by continuing education administrators deal directly with setting agency goals and priorities, but most deal mainly with solving problems and procedures to achieve goals, and priorities are implicit at best. However, effective administrators have strategies for decision making about goals, priorities, and policies. For directors of continuing education, such strategies should provide for the participation of people associated with the agency and parent organization in the process of priority setting (Argyris and Schön, 1974).

Concepts About Priority Setting

Strategies for decision making about priorities should benefit from a broad perspective on the continuing education agency as a system that interacts with its parent organization and service area. Priorities that are set for intended outcomes reflect the interplay of multiple influences and competing expectations, beliefs, and values. In addition to the primary outcome of enhanced proficiencies for adult learners, there are secondary outcomes to the agency, the parent organization, the general public, and even other providers of continuing education. This chapter explores how effective administrators help achieve consensus on desirable outcomes by the use of procedures that encourage actions to achieve those outcomes. The focus is on how program administrators influence priorities, and not on organizational levels of policy making.

Choices and Outcomes. Priority setting entails choosing some objectives instead of others. Because few continuing education provider agencies have a policy board that gives much attention to continuing education, priority setting is mainly an administrative concern. Unlike routine procedural decisions, when administrators decide among objectives they give substantial attention to goals and outcomes.

For example, a director of public school adult basic education may decide to resist the "numbers game" implicit in state education department guidelines that emphasize reaching the most adults with the funds allocated, and instead set aside some funds for intensive efforts to attract and retain harder-to-reach undereducated adults (Darkenwald and Larson, 1980). By contrast, a director of community college continuing education may adopt a policy of responding primarily to requests for courses from the general community and thus be unresponsive to adults from which manifest demand is lacking.

Likewise, a hospital director of continuing education may seek to balance attention to educational programs to increase the productivity of nurses and allied health personnel with programs designed to promote individual career development. By contrast, a business director of education and development may abandon career development activities aimed at long-term employee development in the face of pressure from top management to emphasize short-term remedial activities. In each of these instances, choices are made regarding who will receive continuing education on what topics and for whose benefit.

These decisions deal mainly with the relative priority to be given to various outcomes. Of course, all administrative decisions relate to goals and outcomes to some extent. A decision to rely on printed brochures implies that adults who depend on oral communications for choosing educational activities may not know about them. A decision to hire a content expert who is not familiar with how adults use that content implies that course content may have limited application to adult learners.

However, decisions about priority setting, which are the focus of this chapter, deal more directly with values and outcomes. Such attention to values is more likely to occur when an administrator experiences a change of direction that unsettles the assumptions and rules of thumb upon which most people depend for decision making. As with foreign travel, entering unfamiliar territory regarding clientele, content, or context can encourage administrators to reexamine their beliefs and goals.

Strategies and Tactics. In military decision making a distinction is made between strategic decisions about objectives to be achieved and tactical decisions regarding implementation. Setting priorities entails strategic decisions. In continuing education settings, strategic decisions have many connections. Some of those connections evolve as one choice influences ensuing choices. Other connections are among people who influence or are affected by decision making in organizational settings. For most priority-setting decisions it is important both to make a sound choice and to obtain agreement regarding the soundness of that choice by people associated with implementation and subsequent decision making. It is helpful, therefore, to consider multiple influences on decision making as administrators fashion strategies for priority setting (Allison, 1971; Mann, 1975; Wirt, 1975).

Action, Knowledge, Beliefs, and Values. Decision making entails action, knowledge, and belief. A decision is an action, but its utility lies mainly in the subsequent actions that the decision influences. A decision by a public librarian to work with a director of adult basic education and to extend library services to adult new readers is of little effect unless library personnel follow through to provide materials and assistance of benefit to such adults.

When making action decisions, administrators rely heavily on their intuition, which is based on tacit (or private) knowledge distilled from past experience, common sense, and familiarity with people and the local situation. Administrators also have available organized (or public) knowledge from theories and research about people, organizations, and communities pertinent to administration. It also appears that decision makers select and interpret the knowledge and observations they consider when making a decision on the basis of their self-concept, their general beliefs, and their values and goals regarding continuing education (Sergiovanni and Carver, 1980).

Although values are important in decision making, they are especially important in decisions about priorities, goals, and outcomes. Most decisions about priorities seek to achieve an agreement that some outcomes are more desirable than others. A strong commitment to efficiently serving as many adult basic education participants as possible with available funds almost eliminates the possibility of attracting and retaining many of the hardest-to-reach adults. People's sense of the relative desirability of alternative goals regarding clients, subject matter, or improvements reflects their beliefs about the essence of education, their hopes for a better life for adult learners, and their aspirations for their own career. This applies to continuing education administrators as well as others associated with priority setting.

Many continuing education administrators are optimistic about the possibility of progress by individual adults and society in general. Some writers have emphasized that values such as faith in learning, commitment to adulthood, and fundamental optimism are essential to education in general (March, 1975).

A useful rationale for an optimistic and humanistic approach to administration was presented by Maslow (1965). He argued that administrators proceed from the following assumptions: People are to be trusted and informed, they are improvable, they have the impulse to achieve, seek self-actualization, and grow through delight and through boredom. This approach also assumes that people have good will toward others in the organization, they enjoy good team work, prefer to identify with more and more of the world, have the ability to admire their contributions but recognize their limitations, and like to be justly and fairly appreciated—preferably in public.

Competing Expectations. It may be difficult for administrators to embrace such assumptions, especially when they are buffeted by many competing expectations. It is important for administrators to realize that they have internalized value assumptions that produce the intuition upon which they depend for decision making. Those values are of many types (including aesthetic and ethical as well as scientific, political, and technical) and they relate to the desirability of outcomes as well as the quality of the process (Sergiovanni and Carver, 1980). Setting aside intermittent periods of solitude for reflective thought is as important for an administrator as scheduling staff meetings. Such direct consideration of values helps an administrator attend to moral as well as rational aspects of leadership; to care as well as to know (Eble, 1978). Furthermore, because priority setting typically includes other people, it is useful to deal explicitly with values in the process of gaining agreement on desirable outcomes.

Effective priority setting entails doing first things first and doing them one at a time. Because administrators confront so many alternatives, the best way to obtain results is to concentrate time and energies on major opportunities. Some alternatives are inherited activities that should be pruned if the agency is to remain vital. Instead of bailing out the past, effective administrators put today's resources to work on the opportunities of tomorrow. The process of deciding the objectives to reject as well as those to accept requires concentration of effort and the courage to persevere. Effective priority setting also entails planning so that decisions are not made by default, striving toward important and challenging goals, and emphasizing opportunities instead of problems and the future instead of the past (Drucker, 1966).

Levels of Outcome. When administrators help with priority setting, they are likely to confront several levels of agency outcomes. The fundamental outcome of continuing education is enhanced proficiency of adult learners (their increased capability to perform effectively). In judging the worth of continuing education, most people are interested in the numbers and characteristics of the adults who are served, the extent and types of proficiencies enhanced, and what the participants do with what they have learned. (Of course, some benefits of continuing education participation may be largely independent of learning anything, such as credentials earned, income increased, or prestige heightened). The benefits of continuing education may also accrue to groups, organizations, and communities in which adults apply what they learn. Thus, the indirect beneficiaries of the fundamental outcome of continuing education include the children of participants in a parent education course and the patients of a physician who takes a postgraduate course.

It is important to emphasize the enhanced proficiency of adults as the fundamental outcome of a continuing education agency, in part because this is not the main outcome of the parent organization with which the agency is associated. This emphasis also is important because it is the main criterion against which to assess the success of the agency and to evaluate its effectiveness. These related outcomes may benefit the parent organization (such as public relations or use of underused facilities) and other providers (such as a positive image, or satisfied participants seeking further education). To illustrate why satisfactory achievement of the fundamental outcome of enhanced proficiency is usually necessary for the related benefits to occur, consider that when the public has unsatisfactory contact with a continuing education agency, the typical result for the parent organization is negative public relations (Knox, 1967).

Multiple Influences. In practice, priority setting is subject to many influences, especially because continuing education agencies tend to be very responsive. Because participation is typically voluntary, adult learners have an enormous influence on agency priorities. Plummeting enrollments can terminate part of an agency's program in short order. Those who plan and conduct individual courses and workshops have great latitude in doing so. The influence of participants, resource persons, and program administrators on program offerings is so great that many agencies appear to have no procedures for priority setting at all (Allison, 1971). Agency goals and directions seem to be simply a reflection of the many decisions about individual educational activities.

Examples of Priority Setting. Decisions made within government or within the parent organization can be very influential on priority setting. For example adult basic education programs are conducted by public schools and sometimes by community colleges based on federal subsidies administered by state education departments. The size of a local program mainly depends on the annual state allotment of funds based on the number of participants reported for the previous year. With the resulting emphasis on attracting as many people as possible with available funds, the undereducated adults who are served tend to be the easiest to attract and retain; those who function well in traditional continuing education. It is far more expensive to use the facilities, staffing, methods, and materials required to attract and retain the harder-to-reach adults. A director who did so would experience a declining budget each year as funds shifted to programs with expanding enrollments. As a result, most directors play the numbers game, and governmental policies greatly influence program priorities.

Directors who want to give higher priority to serving harder-to-reach adults can study the recent literature on the subject (see, for example, Darkenwald and Larson, 1980) to find out about concepts and procedures for doing so, recognize that government guidelines give lip service to the importance of helping the hard to reach, discuss this with other practitioners in the state, and propose to the state director of adult basic education on behalf of local directors that state guidelines allow setting aside up to one-quarter of the local budget for intensive efforts to reach and teach hard-to-reach adults and that the annual allocation be based on enrollment related to the other three-quarters of the budget.

Another example of government policies shaping local priorities has to do with continuing education for teachers provided by universities and supported by federal funds. During the past two decades there have been federal acts that contain provisions for continuing education of teachers designed to help achieve the purpose of the legislation. The acts deal with strengthening attention to vocational education, health education, science education, and special education, as well as an emphasis on reading and languages. Universities interested in providing such continuing education could obtain federal funds to do so. Because there was little encouragement to include state education departments, local school systems, or associations of teachers in the process, most of the continuing education programs focused on the teachers as individuals in an effort to strengthen their content knowledge and to enhance their professional development. Recent moves to consolidate such appropriations into block grants to state education departments are increasing the importance of effective working relationships between universities and state education departments. This also is increasing the attention of some directors of university continuing education programs to the improvement of working relations with local schools, teacher centers, and teacher associations. A major result is a higher priority for long-term developmental efforts to improve teaching, for collaborative efforts to do so, and for organization development (OD) approaches.

Relations with a parent organization also can influence agency priorities. The following example illustrates this point. Edgar Schein, in his recent book on *Career Dynamics: Matching Individual and Organizational Needs* (1978), presents a persuasive rationale for providing employee educational activities that contribute to both increased productivity for the organization and enhanced careers for individual employees. He urges that those engaged in human resource development avoid the false dichotomy of an inherent conflict between the individual and the organization and emphasize the symbiotic relationship that can occur when both the staff and the organization develop together.

The director of an employee development department in the headquarters of an insurance company confronted this issue when setting departmental priorities. The department staff was overburdened and confronted many more needs for employee development activities than it could provide. The six-month calendar of educational activities reflected several influences. The director had an idea of priorities for management development, but when the five members of his staff listed and ranked their priorities and then discussed them at a staff meeting, the aggregate list was somewhat different than he expected. A subsequent survey of employee perceptions of their own career development needs, and the viewpoints of corporate executives, also reflected differing emphases. The director's strategy had to accommodate these different priorities.

It appeared to the director that there were two different views of management development in the company. One view, held by some key executives, emphasized management development as a short-term remedy for deficiencies in current performance. Those who held this view tended to veto proposals by the employee development department and others who held a second view of management development. This second view emphasized a longer-term developmental approach to career development. The company's experience with career counseling and the successful experience of a nearby similar company with a career development center helped move corporate management toward a more developmental view.

The director's approach to decision making to achieve this emphasis was focused on the employee development staff, who reported to him, and on the vice-president for personnel, to whom he reported. The staff member whose advocacy area was career development presented a plan for increasing emphasis on career development. After some preliminary parts of the plan were implemented and their worth demonstrated, the director approached more directly some of the executives whose remedial view of management development had caused them to veto developmental suggestions in the past. In the meantime, the director and his staff sought to build positive relations with the potential vetoers by providing effective educational programs to help meet objectives important to them. In the interim, it was important that the vice-president for personnel, who was on a par with the potential vetoers, was supportive of the developmental approach. The director believed that action would speak louder than words and that the best way to avoid having plans vetoed would be to demonstrate desirable progress.

The director's strategy was largely political: avoid early confrontations with the vetoers, emphasize educational activities that they value to win their support, depend on powerful allies to keep vetoers at bay, and strengthen career development activities for managers to the point that the success of the program will be convincing. Another director of continuing education in another setting might have used a different strategy for priority setting.

A director of continuing education and community service in a private community college realized after her first year on the job that there were two colleges. One was the two-year college that most people thought about, with a full-time faculty and mostly full-time students direct from high school who attended classes during the daytime. The faculty was proud of the curriculum and the high proportion of young, full-time students and had hoped for several decades that the college would evolve into a four-year institution. The other was the evening division—the "shadow college."

Many public community colleges have a majority of older part-time students and a one-college approach. Faculty members teach both day and evening classes as a part of their regular teaching load and division coordinators supervise all courses. By contrast, this evening division had become nearly invisible. When the current president had been appointed five years ago, his energies immediately were consumed by urgent financial problems. As he made progress on the financial front he turned his attention to the evening division. As a result of lower academic standards, higher average class size, and heavy reliance on part-time faculty, it had generated an income of three times its operating costs and had provided a much-needed subsidy for the parent organization.

As the president improved the institution's basic financial condition, he concluded that the arrangements for the shadow college in the evening were an institutional embarrassment, but he encountered resistance to change from both the faculty and the former director of the evening division. As a result, he convinced the former director to accept a different job, changed the name of the division, and hired the current director of continuing education and community service.

After becoming familiar with the college and especially some key individuals and groups, the new director concluded that a major shift in priorities for continuing education was desirable, that there was support for such a change from the president, but that substantial resistance from the faculty was likely. The director decided that a deliberate organizational change strategy was warranted, instead of either trying to bypass the faculty or to persuade them. She was familiar with Lindquist's *Strategies for Change* (1978) and found that it contained a clear rationale and useful procedures for a comprehensive approach to the reorganization of the outreach function. The comprehensive approach combined rational planning, social interaction, human problem solving, and attention to political dynamics. A linkage role for the director and key associates would seek to relate a needs assessment and research findings to a process of open decision making and supported implementation. At a state meeting of continuing education practitioners, the director heard about a recent book by Votruba (1981) that provided detailed suggestions for strengthening support for continuing education within the parent organization with special attention to incentives and rewards to encourage faculty members to support and contribute to outreach activities. She found these suggestions very practical and her strategy to change institutional priorities for continuing education are progressing very well so far.

Summary and Conclusions

Directors of continuing education usually want to influence agency goals and directions. However, there are many possible goals and many influences on the priority setting process. In most large continuing education agencies, other people have power to influence agency goals. Effective strategies for priority setting typically include these other people, such as policy makers in the parent organization and in the larger society, resource persons, and the participants themselves. Specific strategies typically recognize competing expectations and values and emphasize consensus building with all that implies in the form of bargaining and compromise. Such strategies may appear more political than rational.

Finance-related decisions usually require attention to both accounting concepts and nonfinancial ideas related to purposes, circumstances, program development, and value judgments.

Resources

A hazard with financial decisions is that they can take on a life of their own. The dollars and cents seem so objective, and the concern about not balancing the budget or not accounting for funds so evident, that it is easy for an administrator to consider financial decisions as separate from educational decisions. Because of this tendency, it is important for decision strategies related to resource acquisition, allocation, and accounting to take into account both the financial concepts and procedures appropriate to the parent organization and the educational setting, purposes, and procedures that the finances are meant to serve.

Resource Acquisition and Allocation

This chapter on decision strategies is in three sections. The first section, which deals with resource acquisition and allocation, presents some basic concepts and examples regarding finances and education that reflect effective leadership strategies. Included are the intertwining of information about money and education, deciding on the extent of cost recovery, acquiring resources, understanding the financial transformations in an agency, and combining the technical and value components of decision making.

The second major section summarizes findings from a recent national study of cost accounting in continuing education for six types of providers: public schools, proprietary schools, higher education, employers, community organizations, and professional associations.

The brief third section presents some generalizations pertinent to decision making regarding financial issues and emphasizes the importance of taking variations among providers into account.

Finance and Education. Some decisions seem to be mainly financial decisions. These include acquisition of funds to start or subsidize a program and allocation of funds to acquire facilities, materials, and people to learn, teach, coordinate, and assist in the program. In addition to the acquisition and allocation of money, there are decisions about procedures for purchasing and cost accounting, venture capital (or startup funds), indirect costs, and cost effectiveness. Also there is the equivalent of money to be budgeted and accounted for, such as free use of facilities or services or volunteer time. Many a continuing education administrator has wished that these financial matters could be turned over to a business manager so that the administrator could concentrate on the education decisions. This seems especially attractive because procedures for handling money and financial records are typically set by the parent organization.

In practice, most major educational and financial decisions are inescapably intertwined. Those decisions that deal with just finances, or just personnel, or just goals, or just program development are relatively easy to make. The difficult and important decisions include joint consideration of goals, programs, and personnel as well as finances and other resources. Continuing education administrators with effective decision-making strategies have found ways to take these multiple aspects into account.

For example, general economic trends such as inflation and rising energy costs have a direct impact on continuing education. Agencies that conduct many workshops and conferences for adults from a large geographic area are especially hard hit when transportation and housing costs rise faster than personal or employer budgets. The problem is compounded when reductions of government funds for social services result in staff reductions and the virtual elimination of agency funds for staff development.

A director of continuing education in a university school of social work confronted this problem. Over more than a decade she had built up a large program of two- and three-day on-campus workshops for social workers and practitioners from related helping professions who worked in several states. These workshops were highly regarded as well designed and very useful. They dealt with specialized topics that attracted practitioners (including alumni from the school) from a wide area and had sufficient enrollments to cover costs.

The director recognized the economic trend and its probable impact on her program as it unfolded. Costs for room, board, and especially transportation were rising, while social work agencies were eliminating funds used to reimburse employees for continuing education. The director's response was to replace the two- and three-day workshops with one-day workshops in several locations within the region. These activities were scheduled on the weekend as well as during the week to accommodate practitioners unable to obtain release time. She also increased marketing activities so as to attract a higher proportion of practitioners from each locality in order to recover program costs with a registration fee practitioners were willing to pay. In addition, meetings were conducted for alumni, and staff development programs were conducted for individual agencies in the region, with faculty members and other resource persons traveling to meet with them. The problem was largely financial. The solution mainly entailed program development and marketing decisions and produced satisfactory financial results and a balanced budget.

Other directors of continuing professional education with large conference programs responded to the same economic trend in different ways. A director of continuing legal education began videotaping one-day conferences held at a university in a large metropolitan area. The tapes were edited and used by specialists on the conference topics, who attended with plans to conduct one or two follow-up conferences in sparsely populated areas of the state, using the tapes for presentations. The specialists served as group organizers and discussion leaders in the outreach locations, and participants had the benefit of edited taped presentations of the most useful conference sessions plus the opportunity to stop the tape, replay sections, and discuss concepts and applications. The discussion leaders were carefully selected and oriented, and the participants in outreach locations had an opportunity to discuss various applications. In contrast, participants in the original "live" conference, where speakers typically ran over, had little time for questions and discussion (Knox, 1980b). In this instance, educational technology was used to decrease costs, increase access, and maintain program quality. A director of continuing education for pharmacists counteracted problems associated with high travel costs by organizing local study groups for pharmacists and by providing reading materials and study and discussion guides, orienting discussion leaders, and suggesting local resource persons.

Extent of Cost Recovery. Cost containment, however, is only part of the equation. Another part is income, and especially decisions about how much of the income is to be recovered from participant fees. Not only do administrators have to arrive at a decision on fee levels, but they sometimes have to present a persuasive rationale for the recommended fee level (and perhaps additional income) to the person to whom they report or to an advisory committee.

Useful points to consider when preparing such a rationale were assembled by Sulkin and Beder in a recent book on adult education issues (Kreitlow and Associates, 1981, Chap. 9). The material explores several viewpoints in response to the question "Should adult education require self-support from learner fees?" Fee support for those who can afford to pay is advocated in the interest of the pluralism and responsiveness of the field. Tax subsidies for much of continuing education are advocated in the interest of equity, societal benefits, and professionalism in the field.

In practice, there are many influences on fee setting. The process of decision making is incremental when there is a history of a continuing education offering and the fee is adjusted from time to time in relation to rising costs, demand for the activity, and fees charged by other providers. However, the process can also be incremental when a fee is introduced for a formerly free activity. A director of an art museum recently worked through that process.

The museum had received a major foundation grant to develop educational activities for adults, related to museum exhibits. Because of the tradition of the museum to offer a few free lectures and of the preference of the foundation, for most of the five years of grant support the continuing education activities were offered free of charge. However, both the museum and the foundation wanted the effort to continue beyond the period of grant support, and the original proposal referred to the introduction of fees toward the end of the grant period.

In addition to creating an audience for exhibit-related continuing education activities that could become self-sustaining, it was hoped that the introduction of fees would reverse the attrition from the self-sustaining art classes that occurred as the enrollment in free activities increased to over 1,000. To prepare users for the introduction of modest fees, brochures mentioned that some activities had been foundation supported but that it was expected that they would become self-sustaining.

The initial fee was about $15 per series, and enrollments were about half what they had been for comparable free activities. During the year, fees were gradually increased to $15, and enrollments continued to be quite stable. Further fee increases are likely in an effort to recover all direct costs, and it is not known yet at what point enrollments will drop again. Enrollment in the art classes has started to increase, but it is too soon to know how much it will rise.

Enrollments have fluctuated more with program content than they have with fee level. Several continuing education activities associated with popular exhibits have had high enrollments in spite of high fees, while low-fee activities related to topics without a history of local interest have had low enrollments. There has been some effort to set fees in relation to the cost of production and the anticipated demand, but the fees have been similar from activity to activity. Clearly the director's strategy has been to approach this series of decisions as a process of gradual organizational change. The long-term goal has been to create an audience for continuing education activities through grant support and to make the effort self-sustaining through the gradual introduction of fees toward the end of the grant period.

Several options were available. Many grant-supported activities elsewhere have waited until the grant ran out to introduce fees, and the programs typically end abruptly because the transition is too great in too short a period of time. A few agencies have used the period of short-term subsidy to experiment with related or optional fee-support activities. This alternative had the advantage of gaining experience with the types of adults who were willing to pay the fees, the types of activities they prefer, and the balance point between fee levels, program costs, and enrollments that result in cost recovery.

Resource Acquisition. Of course, dealing with rising costs and setting participant fees are only two of many financial decisions. Acquisition of resources is an unending task for most continuing education administrators. Included are both financial and nonfinancial resources. Major types of financial resources include participant fees, parent organization subsidies, tax support, external grants, employer financial support, and auxiliary enterprise income. Nonfinancial resources include facilities, equipment, and materials that are contributed, as well as volunteer service (such as occurs in some community agencies and associations). A major way to acquire additional resources is through preparation and submission of a proposal. Buskey (1981) has prepared a helpful volume on grantsmanship in continuing education that contains both guidelines and examples. Additional financial decisions relate to budgeting, accounting, and reporting. Dahl (Knox and Associates, 1980, chap. 6) provides an overview of resource acquisition and allocation in various types of continuing education agencies.

Financial Transformation. When making major financial decisions, it is helpful for administrators to have a broad perspective on the flow of funds through a continuing education agency. External funds are acquired from various sources depending on the type of agency. For example, a public school adult basic education program may be supported mainly by federal and state tax funds, with indirect costs contributed by the school system (parent organization) and no fees paid by participants. By contrast, a public university continuing education program may be supported almost entirely by participant tuition and fees (some of it reimbursed by employers), with some foundation support for innovative programs. An employer's education and training department may be supported entirely by organizational funds, with prorated costs charged to the operating departments of the employees who receive the education.

Once funds have been collected, they are allocated for the acquisition of ingredients that the agency requires in order to function. Included are the marketing activities used to attract and select participants, resource persons, administrators, and support staff. Other expenditures include facilities, equipment, and materials. In addition to allocation of money to acquire these ingredients, some agencies acquire contributed or volunteered resources or services that would otherwise have to be paid for.

These ingredients are then transformed to produce outcomes through the teaching/learning transaction and related staff support. These program development decisions, such as the use of a standardized course or an innovative workshop or the ratio of resource persons to participants, contribute to the quality of the outcomes and the balance between costs and outcomes. In agencies and programs that recover full costs from participant fees, participants pay the fees that return the funds to begin the financial transformation cycle again. In subsidized programs, participant numbers, achievement, and satisfaction are used to encourage those who allocate resources to continue to do so.

Understanding this financial transformation cycle can help administrators recognize the impact that influences or decisions in one phase of the cycle are likely to have on decisions or outcomes in other phases of the cycle (Hentschke, 1975; Richards and Greenlaw, 1972). For example, reductions in subsidies from government agencies or the parent organization are likely to reduce the programs that do not recover their own costs. In order to avoid this, several steps could be taken. Another form of external subsidy may be obtained, fees may be raised for other programs in the agency to create an internal subsidy, contributed resources or volunteer services may replace the subsidy, unit costs may be reduced by increasing class size or reducing instructional costs, participants who formerly were subsidized through external agency support may attain financial assistance directly, or some combination of these adjustments may be put together.

Another illustration of how changes at one phase of the cycle affect other phases of the cycle occurs when the number and attractiveness of competing providers of continuing education in a service area increases. This can make it more expensive to attract participants and staff at a time when the agency is experiencing declines in enrollment and income. Just cutting costs or just increasing expenditures for marketing to attract participants may only worsen the deficit. Instead this may be a time to rethink the distinctive mission of the agency in contrast with competing providers and in relation to the unmet educational needs of various market segments of adults. Decisions about program development, staffing, and marketing then become part of a proactive strategy to deal with the basic problem, in contrast with a reactive response to the symptoms of the problem which could so easily occur.

Technical and Value Components. Effective administrators combine proficiencies regarding technical processes, human relations, conceptual understanding, and value judgments as they work with others to solve problems and seize opportunities. Financial decisions appear to be based on technical procedures and to benefit from the strengths of scientific management such as objectivity, consistency, and predictability. As illustrated by the following detailed example of cost accounting in continuing education, financial decisions are more related to value judgments and specific circumstances than might appear to be the case. Effective decision makers are able to deal with both technical procedures and value judgments as they make decisions that fit both current circumstances and long-term goals and policies.

Cost Accounting

Most continuing education administrators deal with cost accounting concepts and procedures to some extent. A conference coordinator estimates costs and income when preparing a conference budget, setting the conference registration fee, and making commitments for expenditures. During planning and operational stages, cost figures are used to help decide how to deal with additional proposed or unanticipated expenses. After the conference, final income and cost figures can be used for planning if and how subsequent conferences should be budgeted.

Administrators have available useful guidelines for decision making related to cost accounting. A chapter by Gross and Martin on "Cost Accounting in Non-profit Organizations" is especially applicable to most continuing education agencies. (Davidson and Weil, 1978). A forthcoming book by Anderson and Kasl, *Costs and Financing of Adult Education and Training,* analyzes cost relationships for various types of continuing education providers. Its findings provide the basis for the following examples of cost relationships in continuing education agencies associated with public schools, proprietary schools, higher education institutions, employers, community organizations, and professional associations.

Accounting Concepts. Cost accounting procedures are based on a few fundamental concepts. The main purposes of cost accounting are to enable administrators to be accountable for funds and to have timely financial reports available at all levels in the agency in order to make decisions regarding pricing, evaluation, and planning. Many of these decisions entail organizational changes to increase efficiency by producing more agency outcomes (benefits) for less cost. In large agencies, directors can use such financial reports to make decisions about individual courses or workshops (such as recompense for resource persons and the amount to spend on marketing).

For purposes of cost accounting, *cost objects* are the targets of cost analysis and are the expenditures of time, money, and effort related to an agency outcome. Precise costs are ascertained within the context of a decision or objective because sometimes costs can be interpreted in several ways. Although Anderson and Kasl (forthcoming) analyzed the costs of continuing education agencies and did not deal directly with variations in outcomes or benefits, when an administrator engages in decision making in a specific situation both costs and benefits are considered. As in most nonprofit organizations, decisions about outcomes or benefits are mainly value judgments.

In their cost analysis, Anderson and Kasl use participant learning hours as a proxy for outcomes and there is no assessment of variations in the amount of learning or application. Three levels of costs are analyzed: level 1 includes those costs directly associated with providing each course and workshop, level 2 includes those agency costs entailed in planning and administering continuing education, and level 3 includes those indirect costs of the agency and parent organization that are not easily counted in the program budget. Marginal costs are those entailed in adding an activity when a prorated share of administrative and indirect costs are not added.

Attention to cost accounting varies with each administrator's position and decision making, according to Anderson and Kasl. Continuing education administrators accept the accounting system used by their parent organization. It is both typical and desirable in nonprofit organizations that fund accounting is used, in which program budgets and costs figures parallel an administrator's program responsibilities so that periodic reports indicate the extent to which he or she is "staying within the budget." Furthermore, because many continuing education administrators have limited influence on major aspects of costs and outcomes, the extent of financial analysis is also limited so that the costs of such analysis do not exceed the benefits.

Public Schools. With the long history of public school continuing education and the relative uniformity across school systems generally, the great variety in the ways in which public school continuing education agencies are organized and financed seems surprising, even ignoring such agencies related to intermediate school districts or community colleges. Anderson and Kasl (forthcoming) found it difficult to analyze this variety within a single framework for cost accounting. Such agencies are small—typically about 1 percent of the total school system, and few were larger than 5 percent. They are also typically small in comparison with other continuing education providers. Although there are numerous programs in each state, public school continuing education constitutes less than 10 percent of all continuing education. Major programs include adult basic education and high school equivalency and adult vocational education (all supported by federal funds), and a variety of courses related to family life, leisure time, and cultural interests (usually supported by participant fees). As a result, there tend to be two categories of programs: those with a high proportion of federal funds and those with a low proportion. This is masked by the average for all districts of almost two-thirds of income coming from federal funds (channeled through the states) and less than 10 percent from local funds.

Instructors' salaries account for 60 percent of all costs. Materials amount to 6 percent, which is similar to the percentage of the preparatory education level 1 costs in the schools. Part-time staff accounts for 95 percent of the instruction. Their average rate per hour in the classroom is $10, with the range running from $6 to $20. For those costs classified as level 2, administrator salaries account for about 16 percent of total costs and promotion accounts for about 2 percent. As a proportion of the total budget, administrative salaries tended to be low for part-time directors (who typically supervise small programs and often spend more time on continuing education than the proportion of their time assigned to it), and low for full-time administrators with large programs, but much higher for full-time directors with medium sized programs. This relationship is important for general administrators to recognize, especially when planning for the transition from a part-time to a full-time director, when it would be anticipated that the proportion of all costs devoted to administration would peak for several years until the full-time director could expand the program and reduce unit costs for administration.

Although local directors emphasize cost recovery, this entails only direct costs classified as levels 1 and 2. Indirect level 3 costs are absorbed by the school system as a form of in-kind contribution. In exchange for this subsidy, the continuing education program contributes to community support for the school system. Average class enrollments are a major influence on the recovery of direct costs. When using participant learning hours (PLH) as a proxy for outcomes, the cost per PLH (for all costs) is about $2, which is the lowest among all categories of providers.

Proprietary Schools. Especially in large urban areas, there are many proprietary occupational schools that enroll adult part-time students. They cover topics such as secretarial science, cosmetology, truck driving, and computer programming. Many are quite small, and together their part-time enrollments constitute less than 3 percent of all continuing education. Their income is from tuition and fees. About one-fifth of total costs are for instructors' salaries and about one-tenth for materials, so that level 1 (instructional) costs are almost one-third of total costs. The average contact hour rate of pay for instructors is $14. Only one-fifth of the instruction is by part-time staff, but the full-time instructors generate more participant learning hours (PLHs) so that their cost per PLH is the same as or less than that for the part-time instructors. Courses with supervised practice (such as typing or welding) have high unit costs. Such instruction, along with low class size and expensive facilities, are major contributors to high costs. When computing the cost recovery of courses, fee income is expected to be four or five times the cost of instructor salaries.

Because in most proprietary schools a small staff handles tasks related to both administrative (level 2) and indirect (level 3) costs, these two levels are difficult to separate. Profit to owners is also included. Highly profitable schools keep income up and costs down. Detailed cost data are most likely to be available when there are contracts for education with third-party organizations. The average cost per PLH is $3, the lowest except for public schools.

Higher Education. Continuing education programs offered by public and private community colleges, four-year colleges, and universities tend to be quite decentralized. Topics are specialized and related to academic departments. Faculty members typically make major decisions about content and teaching. Seldom does a director of continuing higher education have responsibility and authority for the entire outreach effort. Furthermore, higher education accounting is more oriented toward stewardship than toward decision making. As a result, there is a great variation in the familiarity of directors of continuing higher education with financial relationships. Some continuing higher education divisions are very large and there are many divisions of all sizes in each state, with the result that higher education institutions provide more than one-third of all continuing education.

Almost two-thirds of the income for continuing higher education is from tuition and fees, although a portion of this is indirectly subsidized by federal educational opportunity grants and loan subsidies. The federal government provides only a small percentage of direct income, with state and local government providing the remaining third. Of course, for private institutions, the amount received from government funds is very low and the main source of funds is tuition and fees. Some continuing higher education activities generate instructional credit hours or the equivalent that are used to obtain state funds for the institution; for example, credit courses and some reimbursable noncredit activities offered by community colleges. Although this may not be reflected in the continuing education division budget, it is institutional income generated by the division.

About half of the costs for continuing higher education are instructional salaries and fringe benefits, while almost none are for materials because students buy their own books and use the library (for which the division does not have to budget). The average contact hour rate of pay for instructors is

$20 for the more than three-quarters of the instructors who teach part-time. This comes to about $800 for a semester course. It is more difficult to calculate an hourly rate for full-time faculty members who teach adults part-time, because (especially at research-oriented universities) faculty members have duties other than teaching, and there is little agreement on the proportion of load that was devoted to teaching one course as part of the resident instruction program. Anderson and Kasl use two-thirds as the amount of load for teaching courses. (In a major research-oriented university with much time devoted to research, and with small teaching loads, the proportion of time spent on teaching courses is probably much lower.) The hourly rate for full-time instructors is $45. Administrative costs are about 15 percent, promotion costs are about 4 percent, and level 3 indirect costs are about 35 percent. (It is also difficult to decide which indirect costs are fairly charged to continuing education.) The costs per PLH are $5.

Some of the most important and difficult decisions by continuing higher education administrators are related to cost recovery. Included in this study are considerations of the extent of cost recovery for individual activities and for entire program areas, criteria for full cost recovery, benefits of the division of the parent organization that justify subsidy, and comparisons of preparatory and continuing education with regard to cost recovery. Generally, income recovers level 1 and 2 instructional and administrative costs, but in only half the institutions does it recover all of the level 3 indirect costs. Few public divisions recover full costs, unless generation of state revenue through credit course hours was included. In institutions where the continuing education division did not recover full costs, its expansion is not likely to automatically replace lost revenues due to declining enrollments in the resident instruction program for full-time students.

As many experienced continuing higher education directors know, because noncredit activities require much more program administration time than credit courses (but are more challenging regarding program development tasks), there has been a tendency for credit program budgets in the division to subsidize noncredit activities. Cost recovery tends to be greatest for off-campus credit courses because of the high use of part-time instructors at low hourly rates. In general, there are several other characteristics associated with high cost recovery (sometimes referred to as a positive net difference between income and costs). In addition to location in a large population base, a high level of public financial support, and low instructional salaries due to use of mostly part-time instructors, high cost recovery is associated with economies of scale for larger programs. For example, full cost recovery is most likely to occur when more than 340 courses are conducted and when average class size is twenty or more. Because of the local service area, many community colleges realize (as do public schools) that continuing education helps build public support and may accept that benefit in lieu of full cost recovery. High cost recovery for private institutions is associated with a large population base, use of part-time instructors, and high-enrollment credit courses. Of course, overemphasis on cost recovery can have negative results if other aspects of program development and marketing are ignored. For example, concentration on popular courses that many providers offer, the use of part-time instructors, inattention to sound program development, and shortcutting promotion may reduce not only costs but also program quality and distinctiveness and finally enrollments and income.

Employers. Educational programs that employers provide for their employees are now big business (Lusterman, 1977). Anderson and Kasl (forthcoming) focused on profit-making national companies (and a few nonprofit employers such as hospitals) and on the education and in-service training programs they conducted for their employees. Not included were other large nonprofit organizations (such as government, military, educational institutions) that also conducted in-service education for their employees or that provided by small local employers or educational benefits that reimburse employees for the costs of continuing education offered by other providers. When all these expenses are combined with lost time when employees are paid but not working because they are engaged in educational activities, the total estimate is in the tens of billions of dollars. The annual expenditure for employee education for one large company (AT&T) is about one billion dollars (Lusterman, 1977). The educational activities that employers provide for their employees cover almost every occupational speciality and include ways to increase productivity as well as safety, supervision, and career development. Although surveys report that such programs constitute about 10 or 15 percent of all continuing education, they tend to be underreported and probably constitute much more.

Virtually all of the costs of such programs are paid by employers. Full costs are difficult to identify because the programs are very decentralized and many of them (such as orientation of new employees or on-the-job training) are closely associated with supervision. Anderson and Kasl report separately the expense of lost time from work because the amount can be very great, and there are several ways in which this expense can be interpreted as a cost of education. Especially for educational programs that employers provide for their employees, it is well to keep in mind that costs are defined in relation to purpose and context. This makes cross-organizational comparisions potentially misleading, even among companies of the same type. For example, one company may use employee education for low-level new employees to compensate for inadequate applicant preparation, while another company may emphasize education for management and high-level specialists, to reward and retain very able employees and to enrich the talent pool from which to select future executives. Among the multiple benefits of such education are increased proficiency and improved performance, improved communication and cooperation, heightened motivation, better staff recruitment and retention, and greater loyalty to the employer. Especially because of these multiple benefits, program quality and responsiveness to educational needs may be far more important than costs.

More than one-quarter of all costs are for instructor salaries and more than 10 percent of all costs are for travel and per diem. When materials and other instruction-related expenses are added, level 1 costs exceed one-half of all costs. About 80 percent of instruction is provided by part-time instructors from outside the organization with an average contact hour rate of $60, compared with a much lower rate for full-time instructors and other employees of the organization. (It should be noted that employers pay more for part-time instructors from the outside, whereas most types of providers pay less.) Administrative and other level 2 costs are a higher percentage of all costs than for most other types of providers. The percentage for level 2 costs is about the same as for the costs of instructors' salaries and materials. This is partly because much of the instruction is provided by employees of the organization and only their salary while in the classroom is counted, not time spent for preparation. This is also the case because program administrators in the education and training department handle much of the program development and personal marketing within the organization, which, in a continuing higher education division, would be reflected in faculty effort and the promotion budget for preparing and mailing brochures.

The cost per PLH is $26, twice as much as for professional associations and five times as much as for higher education institutions. Among the many influences on this rate are efforts to change performance and not just provide information, the high rate paid for part-time instructors (especially those from outside the organization), high program administrator time devoted to program development (especially for designing new educational programs), and the related benefits expected of educational programs (such as improved future communication among participants and increased commitment to the organization). Lower cost programs tend to have standardized content and to serve entry-level employees. Other ways to reduce costs include reducing fees to outside consultants and instructors and recognizing that the costs of developing a new course benefit it as long as it is offered.

All of the foregoing cost comparisons ignore the lost time costs when employees are learning on company time. When lost salary and wages for the time when employees were attending educational activities were added up, they totaled half of all of the other costs. In educational programs that do not consider lost time costs, there are economies of scale achieved by increasing the number of participants in an activity or the number of activities supervised by an administrator and thus reducing the unit cost. The lost time costs are so large and unvarying with program size and duration that economies of scale decline sharply.

There are differing opinions among directors of education and training about the utility of accounting for full costs and about the desirability of reporting the conclusions to top management. Detailed cost records are most likely to be used when they are required for billing to outside organizations that contract for education when they are required for charge-back to operating units.

Community Organizations. Many community organizations provide educational activities for the public. Many are relatively small local agencies concerned with health, recreation, the family, aging, and social services generally. Examples include the YMCA/YWCA, family services, American Red Cross, and senior centers. Many are affiliated with state and national organizations. They provide between 5 and 10 percent of all continuing education. Their educational activities are informal and related to organizational purposes.

Only 15 percent of income is from participant fees, which are quite low. About one-third is from the general organization budget supported by membership fees, fund raising (such as United Way), grants, and gifts. Almost half of the "income" is in the form of volunteered time and services. This volunteered time is also a major part of the "expenditures" for instructors, administrators, and support personnel to plan and conduct educational activities.

About one-third of all costs are for instructors, many of whom are volunteers. Instructors are part-time, with an average contact hour rate of $10. For those who are paid the amount sometimes varies with the class size. Materials constitute another 10 percent of all costs, which is fairly typical for most types of continuing education providers. Total level 1 costs are somewhat less than half of total costs. Level 2 costs are more than one-third of total costs. Although a somewhat smaller portion of administrative and secretarial effort is volunteered than is instructional time, this contribution is important. Level 3 indirect costs are about one-fifth of total costs. The cost per PLH is about $8.

When volunteered time is ignored, the total for administrative salaries is about double that for instructional salaries. These administrators do little teaching. High cost recovery and low costs per PLH are associated with large class size, longer courses, a large ratio of volunteers to paid staff, and use of a standardized curriculum. This illustrates how high volume can produce economies of scale. In contrast to standardized courses with little competition, few volunteers, and infrequent revision (such as first aid), specially developed workshops and short courses entail much administrative time for program development and the total cost is high. If enrollment and the number of learning hours per participant are high, the cost per PLH may be quite low. However, if the fee is low, the subsidy by the organization may be high. By contrast, the costs to prepare independent study arrangements may be low, but if the number of participants is also low, the cost per PLH may be high.

Information about cost relationships can be useful when making decisions about organizational goals. Volunteers and participants in continuing education activities constitute an enormous asset to community organizations. Information about their numbers, characteristics, contributions, and potential relationships to other organizational goals and activities can be very useful in strengthening organizational support for continuing education. Information about cost relationships can also be used to indicate impact, justify locations, make staffing decisions, contract with third parties to provide educational activities, and plan for program changes. For example, an agency that expands beyond a small paid staff working with many volunteers and makes the transition to several paid specialists is likely to experience some discontinuities and increased costs (overall and PLH) until program size is expanded so that income is increased and unit costs reduced.

Professional Associations. Professional associations have a long history of providing educational activities for their members. Although they provide only a small percentage of all continuing education, the extent of their effort has been expanding in recent decades and their activities make a special contribution to their membership. The cost analyses reported by Anderson and Kasl are based on data from large national associations.

Almost 90 percent of income is from participant fees with the remainder about evenly divided between volunteered time and the general association budget (which is derived mainly from membership dues). In some associations, it is believed that part of the dues income from all members should be used to support educational activities, while other associations seek to achieve full cost recovery from continuing education. An example of volunteered time is when association members serve on planning committees and conduct workshop sessions without honoraria.

About half of all costs are level 1 costs associated with instruction. Almost 20 percent of total costs are honoraria for instructors, with more than 10 percent each for materials, travel, and other instructional costs. About 90 percent of instruction is by part-time staff, whose average hourly contact hour rate is $35, compared with $50 for full-time association staff members who conducted sessions. This reflects the heavy use of national or regional conferences where resource persons as well as participants travel to attend. Almost 40 percent of all costs are level 2, more than a third of which is for promotion. Volunteered time accounts for another third. Indirect level 3 costs are less than 10 percent. Compared with other providers, administrative and instructional costs are relatively low and promotional costs are relatively high. Small continuing education efforts may receive informal association subsidy, but as the effort expands this subsidy is harder to hide. The cost per PLH is $15; only employers have higher costs per PLH.

Several value judgments are part of decisions that include cost relationships. For example, increasing the number of members participating in continuing education is valued more than cost recovery, which reflects the concern of many associations about member services. Also, the practice of encouraging local affiliates to conduct educational activities by agreeing that the national association will absorb any deficits reflects the value placed on local efforts and on volunteered time. Ways to reduce costs include using volunteers, using part-time instructors and speakers, having a large number of participants for each paid speaker, using regional programs to reduce travel costs, and preparing materials for self-directed learning. However, experienced conference coordinators know that some expenses, such as for prominent speakers, small group sessions, and marketing, contribute to high enrollments that allow competitive fees to recover costs.

Variations Among Providers. The foregoing findings from a recent study by Anderson and Kasl (forthcoming) indicate how complicated continuing education finance is and how much financial practices and relationships vary from one type of agency to another. The summaries for each of the six types of provider agencies contain generalizations that might be of interest to inexperienced continuing education administrators associated with that type of agency. In addition, a review of all six of the summaries suggests the following implications for decision-making strategies generally.

1. Great differences in purpose and context from one type of provider to another should be recognized when applying information about financial relationships. Administrators from one type of provider sometimes go to work for another type. Cosponsorship of continuing education activities by two or more providers is fairly common and increasing. In such instances, it should be helpful for administrators to understand both the similarities and the differences in financial practices and purposes among the several types of provider agencies.

2. Attention to outcomes and benefits is crucial for major decisions related to finance. Anderson and Kasl focused on cost accounting and used participant learning hours (PLHs) as a proxy for benefits such as learning achievement, improved performance, or support for the parent organization. However, an administrator's use of information about cost relationships depends on assumptions and evidence about anticipated and actual outcomes that would be affected by finance-related decisions. For some continuing education administrators, a zeal for service appears to be in opposition to a concern about efficiency. Actually, attention to costs in relation to benefits can enable administrators to accomplish more with limited resources and in some instances to extend resources.

3. High cost recovery reflects a combined attention to benefits, income, and costs. An emphasis on responsiveness to multiple needs and benefits is a central theme in continuing education program development and marketing. With multiple providers serving each community and with voluntary participation, agencies that do not offer attractive, high-quality, beneficial activities are likely to lose their clientele to other providers. Money tends to follow enrollments, since most income is from participant fees. Even for programs that do not depend on fees (such as adult basic education, the Cooperative Extension Service, and employee education provided by employers), the allocation of resources reflects both enrollments and perceived benefits. As Clark (1956) pointed out years ago, continuing education administrators deal with an enrollment economy. Economies of scale (such as seeking a participant/instructor ratio of at least twenty to one) and other cost-reduction efforts help achieve desirable levels of cost recovery.

4. Justification for program costs depends on the distinctive characteristics of each agency and parent organization. With average costs per PLH ranging from $2 for schools to $26 for employer educational offerings ($38 if lost time costs are included), one part of the justification is that people are will-

ing to pay these amounts in these agencies. However, administrators who plan, evaluate, and justify their programs know that a more detailed and persuasive rationale is necessary. Fluctuations in unit costs reflect the participants' ability to pay as well as the availability and willingness of qualified resource persons to teach adults for a given honorarium. Some people teach adults on a volunteer or low-compensation basis because they receive valuable benefits other than salary. Other examples illustrate distinctive dynamics from one type of provider to another. For instance, continuing higher education divisions sometimes subsidize activities believed to be of great public benefit, even if it means covering deficits from the budgets of other activities. Also, high promotion costs for professional association activities reflect a small volume of activities for a scattered clientele, in contrast with educational institutions that have more ways to reach a concentrated clientele.

5. All levels of costs are important for evaluative and strategic decisions. This is illustrated by perceptions of level 3 indirect costs or by what to do with deficits. Many continuing education programs recover level 1 and 2 direct costs for instruction and administration, but few recover full indirect costs. Parent organizations that perceive that the continuing education agency is very beneficial are more likely to absorb small agency deficits as a contribution of the organization, to expect that agency income will recover marginal costs, and to view indirect costs as a contribution of the organization. This is in contrast to parent organizations that view continuing education as an auxiliary enterprise that is tolerated as long as it recovers all costs but that is considered of lower priority than every other purpose for which organizational resources are allocated. (This is partly a result of a perception that continuing education has the capability to recover costs while other worthwhile activities of the parent organization do not.) Continuing education administrators who understand full costs and their relation to benefits are more likely to be persuasive advocates of their agency than administrators who do not and who must rely mainly on their zeal for service.

Summary and Conclusions

Most major decisions by continuing education administrators include financial aspects. Thus, knowledge of financial concepts and procedures is essential for much administrative decision making. Because most parent organizations have standard procedures to acquire, allocate, and account for money and other resources, decision making regarding purely financial matters may seem routine. In practice, effective strategies for making administrative decisions include attention to both educational and financial concerns. Priorities and objectives should guide resource allocation. The following generalizations suggest ways to combine educational and financial concepts and procedures to enhance decisional strategies.

1. Value judgments and local evidence pertaining to outcomes and

benefits are crucial for effective decision making that includes technical information about costs and finances generally.

2. Distinctive agency characteristics should be recognized when interpreting costs and financial practices and purposes.

3. A thorough understanding of accounting and other financial concepts and procedures can reduce the tyranny of fiscal restrictions and enable an administrator to use finances to serve educational purposes.

4. Some of the most powerful responses to economic and financial trends are more educational than fiscal.

5. Some of the most persuasive rationales for the extent of cost recovery are more philosophical than fiscal.

6. Proposal preparation (including attention to objectives, clientele, procedures, current resources, and needed resources) provides a useful approach to resource acquisition within as well as outside the parent organization.

7. Cash flow problems illustrate why it is important for an administrator to have a broad perspective on the financial transformation process.

8. Effective administrators have some understanding of full cost accounting for their own internal evaluation of agency functioning, regardless of the extent to which indirect costs are reported or considered by the parent organization.

*Specific decisions to encourage cooperation from policy makers
and potential participants and resource persons can be strengthened
by the perspective of a general marketing approach.*

Marketing

Marketing decisions can benefit from detailed procedures that have evolved and been refined in related fields such as marketing, public relations, and direct mail advertising. In each of these fields there are objectives to be achieved, techniques to achieve the objectives, and concepts that contribute to a rationale regarding when and how to use the techniques.

This chapter contains four sections, each of which illustrates concepts and techniques available from marketing and related fields that can enrich decision making about marketing by continuing education administrators. They are concepts regarding marketing by nonprofit organizations, promotional techniques, highlights from a handbook on the use of direct mail, and the use of decision trees.

Marketing Concepts

Marketing is an area in which most continuing education administrators make important choices, whether or not they use the terminology and detailed concepts of marketing. Because of the voluntary nature of decisions by adult learners to enroll and persist, and by resource persons and experts to help adults learn, and by policy makers and others to allocate resources and contribute time and effort, a crucial administrative task is to win and maintain cooperation. To perform this marketing task effectively takes a knowledge of motives, of potential benefits, of agency purposes and resources, and of communication procedures.

In an ongoing agency, people find out about activities and some of them decide to get involved. Administrators who have sufficient learners, teachers, and resources may not think much about marketing concepts and practices. However, administrators who lack any of these ingredients are likely to appreciate suggestions about how they can make better decisions to strengthen their marketing efforts. Such decisions pertain to priority setting and program development as well as place, price, and promotion.

Encouraging Contributions. Effective administrators achieve results. In marketing, "results" regarding adult learners means that the agency serves the numbers and types of participants it wants and that they are satisfied that the benefits of participation are worth the time and money they spend. "Results" regarding resource persons means that the agency has a sufficient number of people who effectively help adults learn and that they are satisfied with the cost/benefit ratio. "Results" regarding policy makers means that the agency obtains goals or resources and that those who influence the setting of goals or the allocation of resources believe that the agency is achieving desirable results with the resources and that continued support is warranted.

Such desirable outcomes usually result from a series of decisions, many of a technical nature. Experienced continuing education administrators may make many of them almost routinely. For example, the director of human resource development in a large hospital recently reviewed her continuing education activities to decide which ones to drop and which new ones to add so as to be responsive to hospital requirements as well as staff needs. The review considered program objectives as well as which staff members were participating. In addition to the quality of the continuing education offerings, the review considered the locations and times at which activities were scheduled and especially the ways in which hospital personnel found out about activities and were encouraged to attend. She also learned from staff members who inquired about or participated in her programs what influenced their decision to participate as well as how beneficial the program was. This review helped evaluate her recent marketing activities as a basis for deciding on desirable adjustments in her marketing plan and its implementation.

It is unlikely that she thought of this review as part of marketing. It is even less likely that her efforts to encourage people to conduct staff development activities or to encourage hospital administrators and trustees to support human resource development activities were thought about in marketing terms. Nevertheless, these concepts and practices are the essence of marketing.

Over the years, many continuing education administrators have evolved procedures to encourage adults to participate in their programs or to encourage experts to conduct them. Typically, the process has been quite intuitive. Seldom has the process been as comprehensive as in the foregoing example. However, in some cases administrators have had experience in business before working in continuing education and they have brought their marketing concepts with them. The main disadvantages of this intuitive, trial-and-error approach to decision making about marketing of continuing education are that effective strategies take a long time to evolve and that the intuitive ones may be fragmentary and lacking important elements.

In recent years, an increasing number of continuing education administrators have discovered that writings on marketing for nonprofit organizations apply very directly to their situation with little need for major adaptation (Kotler, 1974). This chapter provides examples of some of the marketing tasks that are encountered and describes some marketing concepts and practices that can enrich decision-making strategies. This discussion illustrates how detailed technical information and well-tested procedures from the related fields of marketing and advertising, when combined with some major value judgments, can contribute enormously to decision making by continuing education administrators. The emphasis is on marketing to attract participants instead of staff or resources. Many administrators have found it helpful to place marketing concepts within the larger context of adult participation and persistence in continuing education and to give attention to counseling concepts and procedures as well (Knox and Associates, 1980, chap. 5).

Value of Responsiveness. The central concept of marketing is that it is a mutually beneficial exchange of value between an agency and its various markets and publics. Continuing education agencies provide education to adults in exchange for participation and money. Marketing techniques can help administrators manage such exchanges so that agency decisions about program development, time, place, price, and publicity efficiently attract and effectively retain the numbers and types of adults the agency wants to serve. This orientation toward responsiveness to client needs is a central theme in marketing. Concern about responsiveness by a program administrator is illustrated in the following example.

Administrators of university continuing professional education programs frequently confront a seeming dilemma between faculty preferences for rigorous consideration of research findings and practitioner preferences for relevance and application of such findings to professional practice.

Many faculty members view presentation of research findings as a distinctive contribution that they can make to practitioners in a professional field. A program administrator dealt with an instance in which the participants in a continuing professional education program did not share that faculty view. The message came through loud and clear in the end-of-course reaction forms; so much so that the administrator decided to summarize the major reactions. The participants wanted to go beyond the reception of conclusions from scholarly analysis and consider how they could apply those conclusions to their professional practice. They appreciated the prestigious and knowledgeable faculty hired to teach the course, but they wanted more attention to relevance and application.

The administrator urged the faculty member who served as course director (and would do so for the subsequent course on that topic) to consider participant reactions and to modify the course accordingly. In this process, the evaluation summary provided the administrator with some leverage.

Continuing education program administrators typically deal with faculty members and others who are specialists on topics on which the administrator has little expertise. This makes it difficult for the administrator to influence decisions regarding program content. One way to be more influential is to use effective procedures for needs assessment or evaluation to be able to present a convincing summary of participant preferences that the faculty can then consider. Another way is to use a process of decision making that encourages those associated with the process to recognize assumptions, alternatives, and criteria for selecting a desirable course of action.

In this instance, the administrator worked mainly with the course director but also talked with other faculty members associated with the course. The director agreed to consider changes, and this was discussed at a faculty meeting. Some faculty members felt that the participants did not understand that course quality should not be diluted for the sake of popularity and that the course should not be changed. However, this view did not prevail.

The course director and many of the faculty members agreed to make modest changes in course content to make it more responsive and relevant to practitioners. This mainly took the form of providing examples to illustrate how research generalizations might be applied in specific circumstances and providing opportunities for participants to discuss such applications.

This example shows how marketing concepts apply not only to attracting adults, but also to serving and retaining them as well. The administrator recognized that she was dealing with two publics: participants and faculty. She sought an optimal match between rigor and relevance. Her evaluation of participant reactions and of the course generally gave her evidence of insufficient responsiveness and provided suggestions for course modification that she could use as leverage to move faculty members who had the expertise and power regarding program decisions that she did not. Course modifications to give more attention to discussion and applications could then be discussed with former participants and reflected in the brochure to help recruitment efforts the next time the course was offered. The administrator could also work with the course director and faculty to help assure that the course was as relevant and applied as it was advertised to be.

Marketing Audit. Writings on marketing contain much more helpful information than an administrator can readily use. A way to help select marketing concepts and practices that seem most useful in a specific instance is to conduct a modest marketing audit. A marketing audit consists of a review of three activities: the marketing environment of the agency (clientele, competitors, and general service area); the agency's major purposes, programs, and organization; and the major marketing activities and decisions of the agency (publics, programs, delivery systems, pricing, and time and place, as well as promotion, personal contact, advertising, and publicity). The main findings of such an audit should enable an administrator to identify major marketing problems and opportunities and to decide if and where to make changes to strengthen agency marketing.

With a clearer understanding of the strengths and weaknesses of current marketing activities, an administrator can identify the people to be involved in the process of decision making regarding the improvement of marketing procedures. Attention can be given to new program opportunities as well as to the objectives of current educational activities; to the segments of the clientele most likely to be interested in each activity as well as the promotional activities most likely to attract each market segment. Effective marketing efforts tend to follow a cycle of planning, implementation, and evaluation to guide future planning and implementation.

Encouraging Participation. An ongoing continuing education program acquires an active clientele and a backlog of past participants and repeaters. Informal comments by satisfied participants can become the main way in which increasing numbers of similar adults learn about the program and are encouraged to participate. If the program is attractive, of high quality, reasonably priced, and if there is little competition from providers, the program administrator may give little thought to decisions about marketing. Under these circumstances, marketing practices tend to be implicit in ongoing program development and to be greatly aided by the enthusiasm and informal communication by satisfied participants. The distinctive program and the oral testimony of people associated with it can be sufficient to crystallize the unmet educational needs of interested adults and to motivate them to participate.

However, one disadvantage of heavy reliance on such an informal and implicit approach to marketing is that enrollments will decline sooner—and a smaller number and more restricted range of adults will be served—than if a more deliberate decisional strategy for marketing is used. Part of the reason is that satisfied participants talk with adults who are similar to themselves. Also, other providers of continuing education discover that the topic and public constitute a program opportunity for them as well, and they acquire a share of the market.

Reliance on informal marketing is least satisfactory when an agency seeks to serve a new audience, especially adults who are hard to reach with educational programs. Successful efforts to do so reflect a comprehensive approach to marketing, program development, and counseling to encourage and sustain participation of hard-to-reach adults. This applies to hard-to-reach members of a professional association as well as to undereducated adults. In such a comprehensive approach, needs assessment (market research) entails direct contact with the target audience instead of reliance on suggestions from current participants or on advisory committees composed of people similar to current participants (Delbecq, Van de Ven, and Gustafson, 1975). Promotional activities should emphasize oral communications with people whom hard-to-reach adults know and trust instead of mainly relying on mass media. Program topics and methods should emphasize responsiveness to the needs and preferred learning style of the potential participants, instead of relying on learning activities that have been satisfactory for easier-to-reach adults. Counseling services can help the new clientele deal with barriers and adjustments that have discouraged them from past participation in educational activities. Successful efforts to attract and serve new audiences of hard-to-reach adults have taken into account both personal and situational facilitators and barriers to participation and attitudes such as optimism that progress through education is likely, as well as rational conclusions that the benefits of participation are likely to outweigh the costs (Darkenwald and Larson, 1980).

Most guidelines for making decisions about the marketing mix in a specific instance refer to people, program, place, price, and promotion. The characteristics and needs of the people to be attracted and served should be considered when making each of the other decisions. The program should be made as responsive as possible to the clientele. The place and time should be selected to encourage participation, which indicates the importance of finding out about client preferences. The price should reflect not only program costs but also client willingness and ability to pay and the prices of competing comparable programs. The promotional activities should communicate clearly and persuasively the messages important for potential participants to receive by using the channels of communication they use.

As program administrators make marketing decisions so that programs are responsive to the clientele, it is helpful to understand the influences on clients' decisions to participate. Many generalizations are available about personal and situational influences on adult participation in educational activities (Knox, 1977). Several of these generalizations can illustrate implications for marketing decision making by program administrators.

One influence on an adult's decision to participate is his or her perception of the relative importance of educational activity in contrast with alternative activities, such as a part-time job or joining a bowling league, which might use the same time and other resources. Information about how clients view the relative importance of a proposed continuing education activity can enable an administrator to prepare persuasive promotional activities.

Life change events (such as a promotion or a divorce) typically heighten readiness to learn and trigger educational participation (Aslanian and Brickell, 1980). Information about major triggers for past participation can be used to encourage similar adults to participate in the future.

Some influences are associated with adults' socioeconomic status and the extent of their past participation in continuing education. Included are familiarity with continuing education, the image of providers, orientation toward uses of education, expectations that the individual should adapt, and richness of resources available to the individual to do so. Administrators can use such information to plan both programs and promotional activities that encourage potential participants to take that next feasible step in continuing their education. Lack of such information leads to the widesperad problem of expecting adults to make a much greater commitment to further education than they are prepared to make.

In addition to choosing messages for a recruitment effort, administrators decide on the communication channels through which to transmit the messages. Some channels involve the use of media, such as radio, television, films, newspapers, magazines, books, posters, and direct mail brochures.

Other channels are interpersonal, such as counselors, organizations, and informal groups. Each of these channels has some inherent characteristics that make it more or less effective for a given message and audience. For instance, print media have permanence and can be read and reread at the client's preferred pace and location, but the client must be willing and able to read. Television has immediacy and the reinforcement of sight and sound, but for some people it is associated mainly with entertainment and not with acquisition of useful information. An acquaintance who uses oral communication can take the listener's background and interest into account and can alter what is said based on listener reactions, but may distort the message. A leader in an organizational setting may be able to invoke sanctions that might either encourage or discourage participation. Administrators should consider these channel characteristics when deciding on a promotional plan.

The effectiveness with which promotional messages reach potential participants is further affected by the perceived credibility of the source of information, by the extent of obligation to the channel (such as to a work supervisor), and by personal characteristics that affect the client's interpretation of the message. Part of marketing is recognizing client perceptions so that messages to them will be as clear and persuasive as possible.

Promotional Techniques

Much has been written about specific techniques for promotion, publicity, advertising, and recruitment that can be used to attract adults to continuing education programs. Such techniques are sufficiently refined as a result of extensive experience and research in the fields of journalism, advertising, marketing, and public relations that administrators can turn to handbooks and advertising agencies for assistance that is directly applicable to continuing education. Decision making regarding a specific technique is likely to produce the best results if it follows well-established procedures for, say, arranging a news conference for a renowned speaker, or placing a series of ads, or preparing a news release, or use of direct mail. The more important and creative decisions have to do with the selection and timing of the techniques to use in a specific instance. This section describes techniques associated with three aspects of promotion. The uses of publicity and personal contact are described briefly, mainly to indicate how they might be considered as part of a broader marketing strategy. Then a more detailed review of direct mail techniques indicates how a detailed handbook can serve as a valuable guide for decision making.

Publicity. Most large agencies have arrangements for publicity and public information, and some have specialists or a contract with an advertising agency to handle the details. Having a public information specialist on the staff provides greater continuity and familiarity with the program, while contracting with an advertising agency places a greater range of expertise at the administrator's disposal and allows the amount of assistance from month to month to fluctuate with seasonal variations in publicity requirements.

Typical public information tasks include preparing news releases, arranging for paid advertising, holding news conferences related to noteworthy speakers or events, and facilitating the preparation of feature stories. This publicity is usually related to individual continuing education activities. Some activities receive much publicity because they are very newsworthy or because a great deal of publicity is required to achieve enrollment goals. In contrast, some of the most significant continuing education activities of an agency may be unknown to people in the parent organization and in the service area, other than the small number of specialists who are served by those activities. As a result, the agency's image may be quite distorted, much to its disadvantage. Some continuing education directors seek to achieve a more positive, balanced, and accurate public image by devoting some of the public information effort to the entire agency. One way to do so is to periodically choose an important but little-known aspect of the agency's activities, select some noteworthy examples, and then publicize them in many ways (newspapers, radio, television, speakers) so that the range of agency activities related to the selected aspect becomes more visible.

Personal Contact. Personal contact provides a contrasting example of promotion and recruitment. It has been well established that adults with low levels of formal education, such as potential participants in adult basic education courses, pay little attention to mass media to obtain information for decisions to participate in educational activities. Instead they rely mainly on conversations with people they know and trust.

Although the use of mass media may increase awareness slightly, it is unlikely to produce a decision to enroll. For example, television can provide public service announcements, appearances on talk shows, and local news coverage of program events such as an open house or awards program. Some printed messages require little reading, such as flyers, posters, and billboards in shopping centers, post offices, grocery stores, laundromats, and churches (Knox and Associates, 1980, chap. 5). The benefits of using such media to attract adult basic education participants is more likely to be that it will be seen by acquaintances and members of the helping professions who then mention the information to potential participants. This is especially so for the hard-to-reach adults. Administrators who know about this two-step flow of communication can prepare messages for the media that encourage recipients to say something to a friend. Current and past participants are ideally suited to this linkage role because they are familiar with both the program and potential participants.

Some adult basic education directors have used paid recruiters to contact potential participants at their homes, work places, or at neighborhood gathering places. Recruiters have been used mainly to attract initial participants to a program in a new location. Unless the recruiters also serve in the program as teachers, counselors, or job placement workers, they have a tendency to provide information that may stimulate a visit to the program, but the expectations and the realities are sufficiently different that only a small portion of those recruited will persist. A more effective means of personal contact is for an administrator to identify and work with people who come in contact with potential participants and to encourage them to perform this linkage role. Some may do so formally, such as employment counselors, clergy, and social workers. Others may do so informally, such as people who work at lunch counters, pool halls, bars, bowling alleys, or stores where potential participants gather.

Direct Mail. In contrast with public information to enhance an agency's image, or personal contact to attract hard-to-reach adults, many continuing education administrators rely heavily on direct mail. For many directors, concern about marketing centers on the numbers, timing, contents, and lists for brochure mailings. In some continuing professional education programs, the budget item for brochure preparation, printing, postage, and lists exceeds the budget item for faculty honoraria.

Administrators of large continuing higher education programs are aware of the many mailings that can be sent each year for specialized programs and audiences. A community college dean of continuing education knew about the various types of mailings that had been tried in her department over the years. A few comprehensive catalogues that had been used some years ago gradually had been replaced by many flyers for one or a small group of offerings.

The need for a decision surfaced at several points. Program coordinators used flyers to reach their highly specialized audiences but became concerned about the amount of work entailed in so many mailings. The mail room complained about handling so many pieces. The dean was aware of the increasing expenditures for the mailings when dealing with a tight budget. An earlier cost-effectiveness study of mailings had produced some useful findings.

The issue of mailings was discussed at a staff meeting, at which there was early agreement about the problem and much discussion of possible solutions. Included were various combinations of advertising, flyers, booklets, and catalogues. The dean also obtained information about mailroom volume and costs, the opinions of potential participants from the community, and the experience of her counterparts elsewhere.

Especially when finances were considered, the staff agreed that for the coming year the flyers should be eliminated and replaced with five booklets. This allowed sending mailings to five fairly distinct segments of the adult population. (Unfortunately the printer was late, which made it difficult to interpret fluctuations in enrollments as the result of the change in mailings.)

The dean was prepared to make a decision if a consensus had not occurred. She also believed in allowing enough time to find out if an innovation works (which was made more difficult by the late mailing of the booklets). She wanted to maximize the number of adults served by her program, but also wanted to consider the other effects of such a change. This is a benefit of talking with counterparts at other colleges and with people from the community.

This example illustrates some of the marketing decisions administrators make either deliberately or by default; decisions about the desired extent of penetration of specialized target markets and decisions about balancing marketing costs against program benefits. The ways in which such decisions are made also reflect a director's use of delegation and willingness to use experts on direct mail.

The following section indicates the types of detailed guidelines available to continuing education administrators as they make decisions about technical tasks such as the use of direct mail. These highlights are from one source, a direct mail handbook prepared by Hodgson (1974).

Direct Mail Handbook

The handbook runs over a thousand pages and contains many examples and tips, along with guidelines based on research and extensive experience regarding what works best in the use of direct mail. The major sections of the handbook cover direct mail basics, uses, elements, formats, production, and controls.

Elements. The basic elements of direct mail are the list, offer, package, and fulfillment. Because so many people move each year and postage costs are so high and the most persuasive message is of no use if not received, the most important essential in direct mail is the mailing list. Whether lists of names and addresses of potential participants are assembled, rented, or purchased, someone must keep them alive.

The offer is the specific action that the recipient is to take, such as enrolling for a conference, course, or workshop. The essence of that offer, and even the tear-off registration form, should be prepared before drafting brochure copy and perhaps a cover letter. Effective copy for brochures and letters is typically clear, concise, friendly, and has a tone of daily conversation. Guidelines for copy follow the "stages of adoption" so familiar to cooperative extension staff—get attention, arouse interest, stimulate desire, ask for action. The entire mailing should be considered a package, including the cover letter (with attention to letterhead, date, margins, salutation, short paragraphs, underlining, and signature), brochure, envelopes (and the immediate impression that they give), and postage rates.

The remaining and crucial element is the way in which the agency responds to requests for information and registrations that result from the mailing. This includes timing and usefulness of the information sent as well as the quality of the educational program itself.

Uses. There are many uses of direct mail, including securing registrations for a course or workshop, reattracting inactive participants, maintaining contact with clients between programs, acquainting participants with other activities provided by the agency, stimulating interest in major events, and keeping lists accurate and current by asking clients if their name and address is correct and if they can suggest other names for the list.

Hodgson's handbook (1974) contains a checklist with over 100 sugges-

tions that would be especially useful to someone starting or improving a direct mail program. Following are some relevant suggestions.
- Use a brief, easily remembered agency name
- Provide high-quality programs
- Offer activities that people need
- Develop a selection of offerings
- Develop activities that build on previous ones
- Price workshops and courses fairly
- Establish an accurate break-even point
- Take all costs into account.
- Promote agency programs continuously
- Obtain news stories and editorial mentions in the media
- Use a practical how-to approach to copy
- Write tight copy
- Write the way you speak
- Use testimonials to promote activities and the agency
- Key all ads to test pull and analyze components
- Personalize correspondence with signed letters
- Repeat registrations are vital to success; keep clients satisfied
- Recognize seasonal fluctuations in registrations.

Lists. Whether an agency assembles its own lists or purchases them from others, there are some basic guidelines that can help make lists productive. Following are some based on the handbook.

1. Adapt practices from experienced direct mail advertisers elsewhere.

2. Adults who have enrolled in educational programs in response to direct mail are stronger prospects than any general list.

3. One quarter of the average list will change each year.

4. About 10 percent of the direct mail budget should be allocated to list development and maintenance.

5. Unless there is a list expert on the staff, the use of outside list consultants and organizations will be beneficial.

6. One person should have the main responsibility for mailing lists.

7. Analyze every list being considered for use.

8. Every active list should be checked and cleaned at least twice a year.

9. Use mechanical addressing.

10. Consider the dozens of sources of names for mailing lists (including past registrations, general correspondence, telephone inquiries, recommendations from participants, telephone and community directories, compiled and membership lists, and list brokers).

11. Work with the post office, such as using their list cleaning service and "return requested" service.

Other Ingredients. There are many other ingredients that contribute to success in direct mail advertising. One is copywriting. The quality of copy is

more important in direct mail than in any other aspect of advertising because a brochure may be the only basis on which potential participants decide whether or not to register. There are guides to copywriting but few people do it really well. Typical suggestions on copy checklists are:
- Get their attention
- Arouse interest (descriptions of the program and of benefits are especially persuasive)
- Stimulate desire to participate (evidence such as qualifications of resource persons and testimonials from past participants contribute to agency credibility and the conviction that participation is desirable)
- Ask for action (close by making it easy for potential participants to take the action desired).

Another ingredient is testing and projecting. A major advantage of direct mail is the ease and economy of testing the potential effectiveness of a mailing and projecting the probable returns. Each element of direct mail can be tested to decide which option to select, or an entire mailing can be tested for results against the record of other mailings. Detailed procedures exist for sampling, comparing treatments, and projecting sample findings to the entire list. As detailed as these procedures are, the recurrent advice from successful direct mail advertisers and consultants is to recognize the importance of good judgment.

Especially in some segments of the field, such as continuing education for scattered members of an occupational speciality, direct mail is acknowledged as the most productive marketing technique. Reading and consultation can enable continuing education administrators with little background in direct mail to readily make sound decisions.

Registration. The main purpose of all promotional activities aimed at potential participants is to encourage them to register and participate. Sometimes decisions pertain to how best to handle the registration process.

A community college program administrator had been aware for some time that the fall registration period for continuing education courses was a madhouse. Over the years, the brief fall registration period was squeezed into the period between the end of August (when many adults in the district were on vacation) and the start of classes in early September. Marketing activities such as advertising and mailing the fall course calendar were concentrated in the week or two before registration. Registrations were accepted by mail or at multiple locations where courses for adults were held.

The registration chaos resulted from a peak load of activity in a short time period, with too little time to advise students adequately and to decide which courses to cancel due to low enrollments. The problem seemed endemic, especially for the fall registration, with an unchangeable starting date for the fall term preceded by the end of summer vacations.

The registration clerk who supervised activities related to registration reviewed for the administrator many of the problems associated with the fall registration period and urged that some solution be found. The two of them, along with a secretary who helped prepare materials and maintain records related to registration and marketing, were the main people engaged in the decision-making process.

The administrator agreed that improvements were needed and asked the registration clerk to keep track of activities and problems during the fall registration period because she kept the records regarding when and where peak loads and problems were occurring. The clerk also agreed to draft a proposal regarding desirable changes in the fall registration process. The most likely solution seemed to be to extend the registration period and related marketing into the late summer. The main concern was that doing so would decrease enrollments.

The administrator talked with his counterparts at similar community colleges that had recently started their fall registration period earlier and they reported that it worked well. He also talked with people who worked in the college's public information office and people associated with advertising and circulation at a local newspaper in his effort to estimate how many people might not be reached if marketing and registration activities began during the late summer. He concluded that extending the registration period was feasible.

It was next agreed that for the spring registration, when there was not the problem of a vacation period just beforehand, an extended registration period would be started to find out how it went. The results were satisfactory, and the registration clerk agreed to try to anticipate the likely adjustments and problems associated with the proposed extended registration period for the fall. The administrator adjusted the budget for the summer and fall to reflect the proposed changes.

The problems associated with the traditional short registration period were sufficiently severe that the alternative of leaving it unchanged was not seriously considered. The main consideration of alternatives pertained to how early to start the fall registration and its related marketing activities.

The decision was made to begin advertising and mailing of the fall course catalogue five or six weeks before registration instead of one or two weeks beforehand and to extend the main registration period by about a week. The results were favorable. Enrollments did not decline. Potential participants had more time to consider and plan for fall enrollments and to have preregistration conversations with college staff members. The cost of printing and mailing the fall course catalogue remained the same, but with the extended period of advertising there was some increase in marketing costs. However, by spreading the mail and personal registrations over a much longer time period, the regular staff could handle most of the work and hiring of part-time help for registration was much reduced.

One feature of this administrator's decision-making strategy was heavy reliance on staff members who were closely associated with an aspect of the continuing education agency. In this instance, the registration clerk identified the problem, summarized records regarding registration activities, prepared a proposal, identified likely problems associated with the proposed change and how to minimize them, and had the main responsibility for implementing the decision. A related part of the administrator's strategy was to maintain an open consultative relationship with his staff so that they would suggest needed improvements and assume the main responsibility for making them work. Such consultation extended to others who could contribute to a plan of action, such as counterparts at other community colleges and someone from the newspaper circulation department. The administrator mentioned Drucker's *The Effective Executive* (1966) as a book that contained useful concepts for decision making especially regarding time management.

Inquiries. Promotional activities produce inquiries beyond registrations. Again, Hodgson's handbook (1974) contains useful suggestions about handling inquiries.

1. Decide whether inquiry handling is a part of agency marketing. If so, organize it in a responsive and systematic way.
2. Analyze each inquiry regarding source, importance, and appropriate response.
3. Respond personally and fully in a prompt, friendly way.
4. Assign responsibility and have a system that is well understood in the agency.
5. Screen copy to recognize what seems to be prompting inquiries.
6. Have a practical method of record keeping to help with both responding and evaluating the relative value of various media.
7. Plan follow-up response carefully, especially for prime prospects.

Decision Trees

Some decisions are not so much a major choice among alternatives, or a series of choices like links in a chain, but consist of various branches in which the next choice presented depends on the last one taken. A graphic way of identifying the major alternatives for a rational decision and considering the consequences of the choices is called a *decision tree*. Figure 1 illustrates how a decision tree might be used to decide how to respond to requests outside the policy or current program offerings of a continuing education agency and to do so in a way that considers the contribution of other providers in the service area. When the request is received, an administrator might ask, "Does the proposed activity call for the present purposes and resources of the agency?"

To use a decision tree, start with the question at the far left of the figure and proceed across the page from left to right, answering each question either *yes* or *no*. Different answers lead to different questions. For example, a *yes* response to question B about priority leads to question D about staff time and interest, while a *no* response to B leads to question E about the likelihood that another provider would respond to the request. The letters followed by ••• are action steps instead of choice points and can be reached by different questions.

Figure 1. Decision Tree for Response to Requests for New Continuing Education Activity

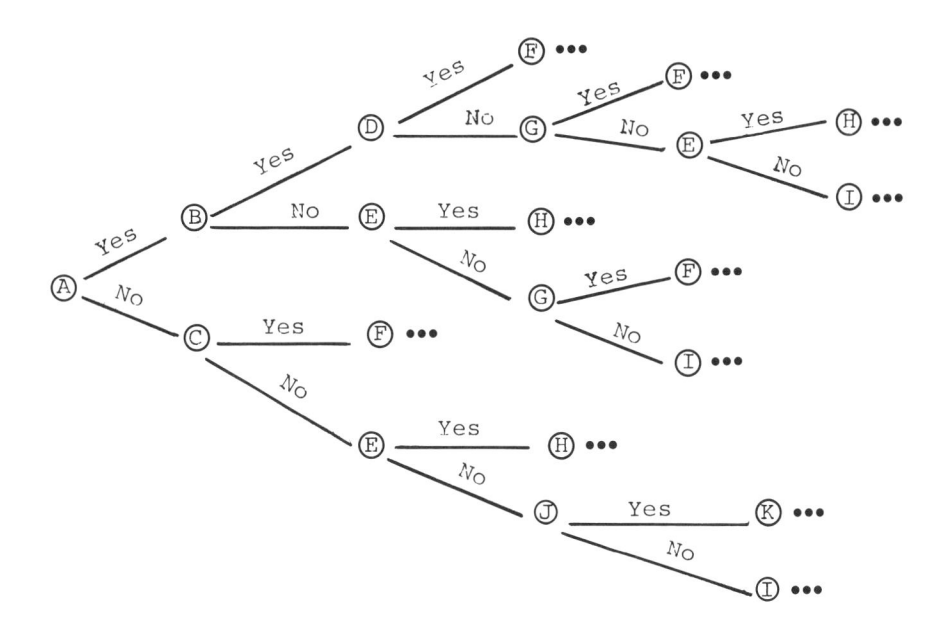

Ⓐ   Does proposed activity call for agency purposes and resources?

Ⓑ   Is it of sufficient priority to innovate, within current priorities?

Ⓒ   Should this be a new agency priority?

Ⓓ   Is staff time and interest sufficient to undertake it?

Ⓔ   Can or will another provider do it?

Ⓕ   Gain support and do it.

Ⓖ   Can sufficient resources be acquired now?

Ⓗ   Encourage them to do so.

Ⓘ   Postpone or refuse.

Ⓙ   Is the proposed activity of high priority for the community?

Ⓚ   Do as trial, then transfer to more appropriate provider.

(••• signifies action steps)

For instance, the series of *yes* answers to questions A, B, and D leads to F and a decision to provide a new activity in response to the request. However, decision point F can also be reached following a *yes* response to question G about acquisition of new resources.

Some decision trees are used to calculate the relative costs and benefits of various choices. This is most likely to be feasible when the variables can be quantified and the type of decision lends itself to a highly calculative model of decision making (Bell and Coplans, 1976; Brown, Kahr, and Peterson, 1974; Miller, 1970). However, some administrators find it helpful to use a decision tree merely to organize their thoughts about a complex cluster of specific choices to make sure that none are overlooked and that a coherent strategy for sequencing and making decisions is used.

Summary and Conclusions

Continuing education administrators spend much of their time trying to convince people to contribute to the success of the agency: adult learners to participate, resource persons to help adults learn, and policy makers to allocate resources. In the process of trying to be convincing, administrators make many specific decisions. This chapter points out the utility of placing such decisions in the context of a general marketing approach and the generalizations available to guide the sequences of related decisions that contribute to an effective marketing mix.

Although this chapter focuses on marketing to encourage potential participants to enroll and persist, the same concepts and some of the same techniques apply to marketing to encourage support by other publics such as resource persons and policy makers. In each of these applications of marketing, it is helpful to clarify the mutually beneficial exchange, to use a marketing audit to discover current practices, and to use marketing concepts to strengthen the effort. Typically, oral communications may be even more important for encouraging cooperation by resource persons and policy makers than for most participants. It is especially important to identify those opinion leaders in the circle of friends and acquaintances of resource persons and policy makers who can most effectively communicate the agency's message.

Because of the complexity of the networks or related decisions that occur in marketing strategies, procedures such as the use of decision trees can in some instances guide the decision-making process, and in general help administrators keep track of the many details. Writings that provide guidelines for marketing generally or techniques related to direct mail can guide the choices to be made, the alternatives to be considered, and the people who should be included in the decision-making process.

Coordination of program development activities can become more manageable by mastering procedures and identifying strategic factors to guide sequences of decisions.

Coordinating Programs

By definition continuing education *program* administrators make decisions about planning and conducting educational activities for adults. Because of their administrative role, their contributions to program development are typically with and through the planning committees and resource persons who make the detailed plans and actually conduct the sessions. This chapter explores decision-making strategies by program administrators regarding coordinating the program development function of their agencies. It does not include detailed decision making about teaching adults, which is the responsibility of resource persons.

One theme of this chapter is that specific contingencies in each situation are and should be very influential on the process of decision making and the program decisions that are made. This is in part because so many people (sometimes with differing backgrounds and expectations) contribute to program development decisions, and in part because some of the decisions include value judgments such as which new programs should be started and which methods of teaching and learning are preferred by participants and resource persons. Generalizations about contingency leadership can help administrators recognize the salient features of a specific situation. Another theme is that there are some technical procedures regarding tasks such as needs assessment, conducting pilot projects, program design, evaluation, and time management that program administrators can help resource persons master (Barrows and Tamblyn, 1980; Foley and Smilansky, 1980; Gagné and Briggs, 1974). A third major theme is that effective decision making regarding program development entails careful attention to human relations, as when supervising the talented people who typically serve as resource persons or when working with planning committees in which major differences of opinion must be accommodated (if not resolved) and at least minimal consensus achieved.

Program Origins

New program ideas and directions have multiple origins, as Nowlen points out in his chapter on program origins (Knox and Associates, 1980). Included are needs assessments, societal trends, and spinoffs from other programs in the agency and in the field generally, as well as the values and vision of program administrators, resource persons, and potential participants engaged in the planning process. The following example of starting a technical education learning center to support self-directed learning by blue-collar adults illustrates these multiple influences. It also indicates how a continuing education program administrator worked through some of the major decisions in establishing a learning center.

A community college continuing education program administrator was asked by the supervisor of technical programs, who reported to him, about establishing a learning center. The supervisor was familiar with the use elsewhere of print, audio, and visual materials to support self-directed study by adults interested in mechanical and electrical technology topics. The administrator was impressed with the supervisor's initiative and enthusiasm for starting a learning center, and they decided to explore the idea further.

Several influences encouraged them to consider additional ways to provide technical education for adults on a more self-directed basis. Included were the shortages of technical workers, less than full enrollments in standard technical education courses for adults, and the availability of money to strengthen such offerings. Concurrent public and media interest in the problems of semiskilled workers, an able and recently selected chairman of the college's community advisory committee on industry and education, and the supervisor's expertise and willingness to help plan and implement a learning center were additional influences.

The program administrator and the supervisor then located another community college that had already established a technical education learning center for adults, and the supervisor visited the site, reviewed the materials and equipment that were being used, and found out about its operation generally. A proposal for a learning center was prepared, indicating the need for a center, its objectives, the use of existing resources such as print materials and correspondence courses, and plans for acquisition of additional resources such as a microcomputer and video equipment. The proposal was discussed with the director of continuing education and the chairman of the advisory committee to obtain their support and funding for the center. The director allocated some college funds intended for this general purpose, and with the assistance of the advisory committee a government grant for technical education was obtained.

The concept of a learning center for technical education was sufficiently persuasive and the timing was right in relation to media interest in semiskilled workers and the availability of government funding, so that support for the proposal developed steadily and no alternatives to the proposal were seriously proposed. There were minor shifts as the proposal was implemented, however. It was anticipated that the main demand would be for the education of mechanical technicians, whereas the greatest demand for education was from electrical technicians. Also, it was thought that the proposed center would be in conjunction with a math learning center on campus, but no space was available there. When some space was located in an outreach location a half-mile from campus, it was decided to place the vocational learning center there.

When the vocational supervisor originally proposed greater assistance for self-directed study, the administrator agreed that this was desirable. The administrator then helped to make the idea operational and to build support for specific plans to implement it. His strategy was reflected in a commitment to varied and responsive program offerings, a participatory style that combined reliance on staff expertise and building support for a proposal both inside and outside the organization, and being alert to the helpful timing of interest and resource availability.

Starting a new program is one of three major decisions regarding products and services that have been analyzed from the viewpoint of marketing of services by nonprofit organizations (Kotler, 1974). The other two decisions deal with program modification and with elimination of programs to be dropped from agency offerings. Kotler suggests that development and launching of a successful major new program involves the following seven steps:

1. Idea generation and screening to identify many program ideas from various sources and to select those that are most promising
2. Concept development to fuse benefits and features in a program likely to be appealing to a target market
3. Concept testing to obtain reactions from potential participants, so that the program can be modified regarding relevance and appeal (this stage is central to market research and to needs assessment)
   a. Is the program purpose clear and easy to understand?
   b. Do potential participants understand the distinct benefits of the program and how it compares with competing offerings?
   c. Are potential participants likely to participate in the program instead of in competing activities?
   d. How do potential participants feel about program attributes such as purpose, format, accessibility, quality, and price?
4. Economic analyses to find out if there is sufficient potential interest in the program to justify further development and launching
5. If there is, then detailed program development proceeds with attention to objectives, topics, methods, staffing, orientation, and materials
6. Test marketing to conduct the program on a small scale to evaluate program performance under actual conditions, to explore market potential, and to reduce risks during widespread implementation

7. Introduction of the program on a large scale.

Of course, such an elaborate process would not be used to offer one course or workshop for an established clientele that was based on experience with programs on similar topics. However, when several national engineering societies were developing a workshop plan and materials to help established engineers master a new procedure, they went through these steps on a prototype workshop before sending it out to be implemented by local chapters throughout the country. Even for modest new programs, these steps provide a useful guide to assure that all of the major decisions are made in a specific instance.

Orientation of Resource Persons

Some of the resource persons with whom program administrators work have little experience planning and conducting educational activities for adults. Thus, one program coordination task is provision of orientation and assistance for experts with little background helping adults learn. The main challenges are to select concepts regarding adult learning and teaching that are relevant and helpful, given a resource person's background and interest in self-improvement, and to avoid being overwhelming (Knox and Associates, 1980). Familiarity with continuing education program development concepts and procedures can enable a program administrator to decide which suggestions would be most helpful in a specific instance. Effective administrators have benefitted from overviews of program development such as Houle, *Design of Education* (1972); Knowles, *The Modern Practice of Adult Education* (1980); and Knox and Associates, *Developing, Administering, and Evaluating Adult Education* (1980).

Pennington and Green (1976) confirmed what many experienced administrators assumed—that much program development is quite intuitive and draws little upon research and experience by others. Because the resource persons with whom program administrators work are experts in their fields, many are responsive to specific ideas about how to enrich the ways they plan and conduct educational activities for adults. One way to generate ideas is for the administrator and resource person to identify a planning or teaching procedure that seems unsatisfactory, decide on a way to accomplish the objective effectively, and then adapt the suggestions of others to the specific situation. For example, recent overviews are available on needs assessment (Pennington, 1980), reaching hard-to-reach adults (Darkenwald and Larson, 1980), teaching adults effectively (Knox, 1980a), and program evaluation (Knox and Associates, 1980; NJCSEE, 1981).

Deciding *how* to provide useful ideas about helping adults learn also depends on specific circumstances. In some instances it is only possible to use a brief conversation (when making arrangements or between workshop sessions) or a short pamphlet (Bock, 1979) distributed to inexperienced teachers of adults. In other instances, resource persons would be willing to read such a pamphlet, or a more detailed overview of teaching adults effectively (Knox, 1980a) and then attend one or two orientation sessions to discuss how the suggestions could be used to strengthen practices they want to improve. Sometimes the most useful ideas pertain to self-directed learning (Knowles, 1975; Knox, 1974). Sometimes interest would be greatest in program development related to organization development (Beckhard, 1969; Bennis, 1969; Varney, 1976). In an increasing number of instances, program administrators want to help teachers of adults attend to both individual and organizational needs (Johnson, 1978; Schein, 1978; Suter and Green, 1981). Effective administrative decisions depend on an understanding of the specific situation and on pertinent organized knowledge that could contribute to improved performance.

Planning Committees

Planning committees are widely used by administrators to guide program development. Such committees enable administrators, resource persons, and representatives of potential participants to agree on mutually satisfactory plans for program objectives and procedures. An ability to call and conduct meetings can help an administrator to involve those who should contribute to program decision making. The calling of meetings is facilitated by making sure that a meeting is necessary for the purpose; by agreeing on committee objectives and procedures; by scheduling meetings that are optimal in number, duration, day, time, and location; and by preparing in advance. The conducting of meetings is facilitated by clarifying session objectives, by accomplishing necessary tasks efficiently but with fairness and concern, by producing worthwhile results, and by ending at a reasonable time (Eble, 1978; Prince, 1970). As in most other group activities, effective committee leadership entails producing worthwhile results along with member satisfaction.

However, those who chair successful planning committees make decisions that extend beyond calling and chairing meetings. Such additional decisions are enhanced by an understanding of important and timely issues to address in the educational program, of effective program development procedures, of tasks performed well by committees and tasks best handled in other ways, and of how to handle a series of intergroup decisions that produce agreement on a sound continuing education program plan. The three groups that should be included in decision making are resource persons, potential participants, and administrators. When one of these groups is not represented on the planning committee, provision is sometimes made to obtain its contribution indirectly, such as needs assessment information from potential participants or proposed topics and activities from potential resource persons.

In the process of joint decision making, planning committees typically agree on at least the following four general decisions:
  1. the probable clientele, including assumptions about their numbers, educational needs, and likelihood of participation;
  2. the appropriate type of program, including program objectives and benefits, teaching-learning activities, and an evaluation plan;

3. specifications for resource persons (including expertness and effectiveness in helping adults learn), and suggestions of people who might help conduct the program; and
4. the cluster of time, place, and financial arrangements.

In practice, planning committees sometimes make specific choices of mailing lists, themes, speakers (who then decide on objectives, activities, and evaluation), and time and place. The coordinator lets them know whether they've overspent their budget or what the fee should be to recover costs, and adjustments are made if needed. Alternative goals or ways to achieve them may not be considered. For a committee that works well together and plans the next year's conference in a continuing series with a well-established tradition, it may not be necessary for the chair to give much attention to intergroup relations. However, when committee members have differing expectations about planning a new program, an understanding of group dynamics is helpful to a committee chair. This is especially true when members have agreed to make a joint decision but are unable to agree on a plan.

Three influences on the extent to which committee members recognize a need for joint decision making are the apparent similarity in their initial conceptions of the educational program, their perceived mutual dependence, and their assessment of the need for and possibility of controlling planning. Members whose needs for control are low, whose initial conceptions of the program are different from the other members', and whose perceived interdependence is high are likely to recognize the need for joint decision making. However, if they do *not* perceive an interdependence and the initial program conceptions are very similar, they will probably favor the delegation of authority for decision making to one person—themselves if they have a high need to control, or someone else if they have a low need to control and if the other person is perceived as competent.

Both the apparent similarity of initial program conception and the perceived mutual dependence among committee members tend to occur when there is a history and established pattern of communication among members and some clarity in the members' goals for the program. Communication among members is facilitated by few members, many opportunities to interact, enough resources available to facilitate planning (such as travel funds and a telephone and correspondence budget), and a clear conception of effective planning procedures derived from outside materials or a resource person. Clarity of program goals is facilitated by members' abilities to articulate their orientation regarding the purposes that continuing education can serve. Two additional conditions that facilitate a perceived mutual dependence among committee members are the perception that other members can make important and complementary contributions and the members' own willingness to collaborate.

Three conditions contribute to a member's assessment of the need for and possibility of controlling planning. One is the degree to which the member needs to control the activities in which he or she takes part. A second is the member's self-confidence based on felt acceptance in both the continuing education planning committee and related reference groups (such as a faculty group for a resource person, a cosponsoring association for a representative of the clientele, or an agency staff for the program administrator). A third condition is the member's personal involvement related to program planning. Members would be expected to feel involved to the extent to which they view the planning committee as a means of achieving personal and/or social goals related to the program and to which they are committed. A commitment to social goals related to the program might also result in personal involvement in program planning, even though the member might not view the planning group as a likely means of achieving the goals.

A coordinator who chairs a planning committee in which difficulty with joint decision making is part of the problem can use such insights to understand interpersonal dynamics, achieve consensus, select appropriate procedures, and generally help committee members make decisions they will help implement. Often, the general policy decisions made by planning committees then guide specific decisions delegated to members or to others.

Coordinator's roles in planning committees are also influenced by what they value. Deppe (1969) found that university conference coordinators serve as boundary definers for the institution as they decide which programs to select or initiate. Personal values are reflected in the relative emphasis on five orientations, of which one tends to predominate for a coordinator. The orientations are toward serving clients, having smooth procedures, creating a favorable institutional image, achieving institutional purposes, or solving social problems. Such values are reflected in the outcomes or procedures that are emphasized in the flow of the decision-making process.

Supervision

The decisions that the coordinator made might have been aided by information from several sources. One (Knox, 1980a) is on procedures for helping teachers help adults learn. Included are both generalizations about adult learning and teaching and techniques for encouraging teachers so that recognition of discrepancies can serve as vehicles for their growth as teachers of adults. Another source (Caplow, 1976) is on supervisory procedures that encourage productivity. This book emphasizes indirect supervision in which supervisors use a focus on desirable and attainable objectives and on fiscal controls, combined with effective working relationships and on amount of latitude that encourages members to be productive. Hackman, Lawler, and Porter (1977) describe work enrichment procedures that increase productivity through participation in decision making and feedback regarding performance. An additional source (Steinmetz, 1969) discusses ways to manage marginal and unsatisfactory performance, including procedures for deciding whether to try to salvage a marginal employee, for helping unsatisfactory staff members to improve if they are promising, and for terminating those who are not. Some adaptation would be required for the coordinator to apply these procedures to a part-time teacher of adults. In general, effective coordinators are more like talent managers than top sergeants; more like directors of volunteers in hospitals than chiefs of staff.

Supervising is the most widely recognized of all administrative roles. Especially in continuing education, it includes attention to the decision-making process in which others take part. However, from his in-depth studies of what administrators in various fields actually do, Mintzberg (1973) identified nine other administrative roles that relate in various ways to decision making.

The supervisor role includes tasks in which the administrator is leader of an internal group (such as a planning committee for a coordinator or the conference coordinators for a director of conferences). These tasks include selecting and orienting staff and encouraging and helping them to perform well. An understanding of effective program development is an important part of helping others make sound program development decisions. The supervisor role is one of three interpersonal roles identified by Mintzberg (1973). The other two are oriented outside the agency. The figurehead role includes representing the agency in routine legal or social ways such as speaking to community groups and signing certificates. The liaison role includes working with an evolving network of people who represent outside groups to which the agency relates. The contacts can be by phone, mail, or in person. Examples include membership on a local council or round table or in a state or national association of continuing education providers, or contacts with representatives of organizations that might support or cosponsor continuing education activities. Other examples include serving as a member of the administrative cabinet of the major administrator of the parent organization to whom the director of continuing education reports (such as the superintendent of schools, vice-president for personnel, or academic vice-president of the university), and chairing a council of people who coordinate continuing education elsewhere in a large parent organization with decentralized responsibility for continuing education. Many figurehead and liaison tasks are routine, but they establish the interpersonal contacts so that when decisions relevant to continuing education emerge, sometimes suddenly, the director is likely to be involved (Cohen and March, 1974). Also, as Knox (1980b) found in the administration of university continuing professional education offices, organizational vitality is associated with effectively performing the combination of supervisor and liaison roles.

A second cluster of three administrator roles identified by Mintzberg (1973) is informational. They are monitor, disseminator, and spokesperson. The monitor role includes obtaining external information (in part through the liaison role) from contacts, peers, and experts, and internal information (in part through the supervisor role) from subordinates. The administrator (and sometimes his or her secretary) then acts as the nerve center for the agency to channel information to others. In the disseminator role, the administrator transmits information to members of the agency, some of it factual and some involving interpretation of diverse values. In the spokesperson role, the administrator transmits information to outsiders, such as announcing plans or giving oral or written reports. Effective administrators also use this flow of information to identify problems and opportunities and to make plans for strengthening the agency and its contribution. It is in the administrative role as strategy maker that the cluster of informational roles is most closely connected with the third cluster of four decisional roles.

Decision making is central to administration and effective directors of continuing education are typically involved in the major decisions made in their agency. However, in contrast with idealized models of rational and goal-maximizing decision making, most able adminisrators "satisficed" or muddled through by accepting courses of action that were merely satisfactory rather than the best. The four decisional roles identified by Mintzberg (1973) were entrepreneur, disturbance handler, resource allocator, and negotiator.

Heavy emphasis on the entrepreneurial role helps distinguish the continuing education administrator from those who administer other types of educational programs. Entrepreneurial tasks include searching the agency and its service area for opportunities for new program directions, initiating improvement projects, and supervising the design of some projects. Examples include providing special programs to serve hard-to-reach adults (Darkenwald and Larson, 1980), using technology for teaching adults at a distance (Chamberlain, 1980), and strengthening incentives for members of the parent organization to conduct educational activities for adults (Votruba, 1981). Writings on organizational change that emphasize multiple influences are especially valuable to guide decision making by administrators who help initiate or design such improvement projects (Lindquist, 1978; Votruba, 1981).

The disturbance-handler role is visible when it is activated and can temporarily preempt other more important roles. Able administrators have sufficient resilience in their commitments and working relationships to respond satisfactorily to crises without greatly damaging ongoing activities. Examples of unexpected disturbances are a deficit due to a sudden drop in external funding, having to replace resource persons or staff members on short notice, or sudden enrollment declines due to new providers in the service area.

The resource-allocator role includes making budget allocations, scheduling time, delegating projects, and authorizing decisions by others. These decisions are cumulative in that implicit priorities within the agency sometimes emerge as a result of the combination of budget allocations, initiation of new activities, delegation of responsibilities, and assignment of personnel time. In agencies dependent upon cost recovery activities, program administrators may largely shape their own future, and directors may, in fact, allocate few resources.

The negotiator role includes representing the agency when negotiating with internal and external groups. An internal example is working out greater academic decentralization within departments in continuing higher education while retaining administrative centralization. An external example is working out details on a collaborative arrangement between a community college and underlying school districts on program offerings and use of school space.

One way of conceptualizing administrative style is by identifying which of the foregoing roles are emphasized. For example, the political administrator might emphasize spokesperson and negotiator roles in contrast with the "store-tender" who might emphasize resource allocator and supervisor roles. However, the work of most administrators is characterized by interpersonal relations, oral communications, and many brief activities.

Situational Influences

For most administrators, more than one-half of their activities (deskwork sessions, phone calls, meetings) last less than nine minutes and fewer than one in ten lasts more than an hour (Mintzberg, 1973). This, combined with the commitment of most administrators to be accessible to staff and to the public and to be responsive to problems as they arise, means that most administrators struggle with time managment problems. The many how-to-do-it books and articles on time management during the past decade reflect the universality of this concern among administrators. However, the essentials of time management have been known and practiced by effective administrators over the years (Drucker, 1966). These include recording time use to identify and prune time wasters and consolidating discretionary time and allocating and scheduling it in relation to task importance. Otherwise, "administrivia" squeezes out time for exploring and planning new directions. As a result, decision making is by reaction and default instead of by a process of deliberate choice over which the administrator has some influence.

Competing time demands and the preferences of oneself and others also influence the amount of attention that is given to a program development task such as evaluation.

A program administrator in a medical school office of continuing education confronted a decision about the type of evaluation for a postgraduate course for physicians. Although not a physician and without much background in the course specialty, she had much preparation and experience in continuing education of health professionals, including evaluation procedures.

The course was a new continuing education offering on an advanced and specialized topic, and it was aimed at a small number of potential participants. The administrator wanted to arrange for course evaluation to decide how well it fit the participants, whether to offer it a second time, and, if so, whether it should be modified.

Substantive responsibility rested with the course director, who was a clinician with little familiarity with educational planning and evaluation but who was open to suggestions. The administrator discussed with the course director the type of evaluation to use, and he had no preference. They raised the question with the dean and with faculty members who were to teach the course, but it was clear that it was up to the administrator and the course director what type of evaluation to use.

They agreed that in this instance the course evaluation would consist mainly of two forms: one at the beginning of the course to obtain information about participant backgrounds and expectations, and a standard evaluation form (with a few items specifically for the course) at the end of the course that would allow a comparison of responses with those from other courses.

There was some discussion of including a more detailed and intensive evaluation of the intent of participants to modify their clinical procedures as suggested by the course, as well as a pretest and posttest and a follow-up study of actual changes in practices. When the administrator considered limited time and money and her perception of how much evaluation the course director would actually use, these other alternatives were set aside. Her evaluation report was a one-page letter of highlights from the findings along with a discussion about offering the course again.

The administrator felt that it was useful to have a strong background in adult learning and program development so that she could contribute to course planning and be flexible in negotiating with the course director, who was a content specialist, an evaluation plan that fit the specific circumstances. She had also taken a course on decision making for clinicians to help them understand the use of decision trees as a way of involving patients as well as other health professionals in the decision-making process. This course on decision making suggested ways to enable her and the course director to jointly consider alternative education procedures and to agree on implementation of an evaluation plan to which they were both committed.

This example illustrates one way in which administrators take into account external and situational influences as they make decisions. This is especially important for the turbulent environments characterized by much change and uncertainty in which most continuing education administrators function (Lawrence and Lorsch, 1969).

A useful distinction when deciding on the administrative approach most likely to be effective in a specific situation is the relative emphasis on task achievement and productivity versus relationships with the people involved and their satisfaction (Blake and Mouton, 1964). Many administrators have found that a managerial grid composed of these two variables (task achievement and member satisfaction) is a useful way to diagnose their own administrative style or even to explore the relative emphasis on task versus relationships that seems desirable in a specific situation.

One problem of relating style to situation is that there are so many situational influences. In his study of group leadership, Fiedler (1967) identified three influences on administrative effectiveness that deserve attention. One influence is the quality of relations between the leader and members (good, moderate, poor). Another is the nature of the task to be accomplished (structured or unstructured). The third is the power or position of the leader in relation to the group (strong or weak). These three variables can be combined to produce the eight situations presented in Table 1 that vary in extent of favorableness to the leader. Favorableness is the extent to which the leader can influence achievement of group tasks.

In Table 1, the eight vertical columns represent typical situations. Situations 1 through 3 on the left side of the table tend to be very favorable to the leader, situations 4 through 7 moderately favorable, and situation 8 unfavorable. The top horizontal row of Table 1 lists the leadership styles that Fiedler found to be most effective in each of the eight situations. Task-oriented styles were most effective in situations 1, 2, 3, and 8, while relation-oriented styles were most effective in situations 4, 5, 6, and 7. In addition to suggesting decision-making approaches or even criteria for the selection of administrators to increase effectiveness in specific situations, the idea of contingency leadership has the heuristic value of helping administrators think about which aspects of a specific situation should be given special attention during the decision-making process.

The concern of continuing education administrators about influencing outcomes includes relations with the parent organization. Usually people in the parent organization are very powerful and make major decisions about priorities, policies, and resource allocation, including release of staff time to support continuing education. The first chapter of Votruba's (1981) book on strengthening internal support for continuing education examines the interplay between the agency and the parent organization and the many points at which influence occurs. Differences among parent organizations are thus important for administrators to consider in the process of decision making. Continuing professional education provides an example.

Knox (1980) found that program development decisions of continuing higher education administrators differ from one professional field to another. For example, low practitioner interest in law faculty contributions combined with low perceived personal benefits of doing so by most law professors and a willingness of specialist practitioners to conduct continuing education courses without honoraria contribute to having almost all continuing education courses of law schools conducted by practitioners, with little involvement by law professors. In contrast, most continuing education courses provided by medical schools are conducted by professors of medicine who depend on referrals from course participants of patients with specialized health problems (which are so necessary for teaching and research purposes).

Summary and Conclusions

Coordinating 40 conferences a year or supervising 200 evening courses can be very complicated. Effective program administrators find ways to simplify this complexity and still produce high-quality programs. They do so by understanding important strategic factors in each situation and avoiding becoming lost in the details.

Table 1. A Summary of Fiedler's Contingency Theory of Effective Leadership

Effective Leadership Style	Task	Task	Task	Relation	Relation	Relation	Relation	Task
	Very Favorable to the Leader				*Moderately Favorable to the Leader*		*Unfavorable to the Leader*	
Situation	1	2	3	4	5	6	7	8
Leader-member relations	Good	Good	Good	Moderate	Moderate	Moderate	Moderate	Poor
Task Structure	High	High	Low	Low	High	High	Low	Low
Position power	Strong	Weak	Strong	Weak	Strong	Weak	Strong	Weak

Source: Sergiovanni, T. J., Burlingame, M., Coombs, F. D., and Thurston, P. W. *Educational Governance and Administration.* Englewood Cliffs, N.J.: Prentice-Hall, 1980, p. 87.

One way for a program administrator to do this is to have mastered program development procedures in order to efficiently guide and assist resource persons who have limited experience with helping adults learn. An administrator with expertise in needs assessment, objective setting, designing learning activities, evaluation, and working with planning committees can be very flexible and effective when dealing with specific people and situations involved with developing an educational program for adults. By contrast, having a limited repertoire of intuitive program development procedures leads to either rigidity or lack of leadership because the administrator is unable to adapt to the specific situation. Therefore, one way in which an inexperienced program administrator can enhance decision-making strategies is by becoming sufficiently familiar with program development concepts and procedures to contribute to shared decision making and to suggest useful references where appropriate.

However, reading about program development is not sufficient. In the best practice, the planning process is very interactive and success depends on effective interpersonal relations. Such success begins with getting along with people and proceeds to the mastery of procedures for shared decision making. Guidelines for indirect supervision, working with planning committees, or recognizing multiple administrative roles can help inexperienced program administrators think through a strategy in a specific instance and avoid troublesome oversights. As with experts in any field, more experienced administrators who are coordinating a familiar program seldom use formal checklists but deal more flexibly with the flow of decisions to be made.

Each specific situation has its own contingencies and involves people with personal values, and effective administrators take these into account. These influences include benefits anticipated by collaborators, clarity and agreement on program purposes, working relationships among collaborators, and environmental influences such as resources and competitors. Frequently the crucial influences and considerations can be lost in a sea of details, but effective administrators can identify crucial aspects to consider in their decision-making strategies. This includes whom to include and distinctive contributions they can make, as well as the ideas and options to consider.

Decision making regarding staff selection and orientation calls for attention to both productivity and satisfaction as coordinators serve as managers of talent.

Staffing

Most continuing education agencies are results-oriented. Productive agencies that provide effective programs for adults tend to prosper and those that don't do not. Staffing decisions are among the most influential on results because the people who work for an agency affect the process of making most of the decisions.

An agency staff reflects decisions about whom to select and whom to let go. It also reflects supervisory and staff development activities. This chapter reviews concepts and practices related to these aspects of staffing. It also considers the division of responsibilities and assignment of tasks for individual staff members and for the entire agency, along with the different decisional strategies related to each.

A point of view is also presented in which supervision and staff involvement in decision making is approached as an aspect of teaching. In this approach, a major administrative role is as a manager of talent with informal experiential education ways of relating to the staff. Staff participation in decision making and in self-directed learning projects also helps members learn how to perform their roles in helping adults learn.

Termination

Few decisions that continuing education administrators make are as seemingly simple, but actually as complex and revealing, as firing a staff member. The formal termination of employment usually involves letting administrative staff go because those who teach adults typically do so as a part-time and temporary arrangement, and a resource person whose performance is unsatisfactory is just not asked to teach again. However, a full-time program administrator whose work seems to be unsatisfactory can pose a difficult decision-making problem, especially if there are mixed signals.

This problem is illustrated by the experience of a director of community college continuing education who noticed indications that her coordinator for community service might not be performing satisfactorily. The coordinator supervised most of the noncredit continuing education activities that were administered by the continuing education division on a cost-recovery basis. She was appointed coordinator two years before the director joined the community college staff, and at that time the community service program was in the red and the director's predecessor had emphasized the urgency of recovering all direct costs. The coordinator was selected in part because, although inexperienced in continuing education, she appeared to be sufficiently professionally ambitious and personally assertive to tackle this demanding assignment. In fact, during her first year in the position, she pruned many of the activities that lost money and negotiated higher fees for most of the remaining activities, so that her second year's budget was close to breaking even. But she paid a price.

When the new director took over, she was impressed with the coordinator's "no nonsense" approach to program coordination. However, during the director's first year, she began to notice little indications that all was not well in the community service program. Secretaries complained about unfairness of assignments, faculty members complained about broken promises, and community members complained about abrasiveness when working out program arrangements. At first the director assumed that these were unavoidable consequences of doing a difficult job. But when the static increased and program cost recovery began to decrease, she decided that something must be done.

She began by reviewing both impressions and evidence about the strengths and weaknesses of the coordinator's performance, the likelihood that a more satisfactory replacement could be obtained, her estimate of the coordinator's potential for improvement, and procedures for termination with due process if it came to that. Based on this review, the director pondered how serious the problem seemed to be and what possible courses of action were available. She discussed the matter confidentially with the associate director, to whom the coordinator reported, and concluded that the problem was serious and should be discussed with her.

The two of them met with the coordinator to discuss their impressions of her performance. Although relevant information was in her reports on community service activities and had been discussed with the associate director, it seemed best to begin with a few major indications that her performance might be improved and then to encourage the coordinator to discuss her current and desired performance. She was moderately defensive during the initial conversation, but at a subsequent meeting all three agreed on several major targets for improvement, arrangements to help her improve the community service program, and the basis on which it would be decided that satisfactory progress was occurring. The associate director confirmed this understanding in a brief memo to the coordinator. The associate director and the director agreed that it had been a good idea for both of them to meet with the coordinator.

After a few months it appeared that satisfactory progress was not occurring. The associate director concluded that, in spite of the coordinator's commitment to high-quality programs and recovery of direct costs, her inadequate use of the program development procedures and abrasive interpersonal relationships were alienating some of the office staff, faculty members, and representatives of community groups whose cooperation was important for her success. This contributed to declining participation and a growing deficit.

The three met again and after discussing the situation agreed to a six-month trial period, including procedures for evaluation of performance and for deciding whether or not to terminate employment at the end of that period. Again, the highlights of the meeting were confirmed in a memo. Before that meeting, when the director raised the question of proceeding directly to a terminal appointment, the associate director mentioned that the coordinator was divorced with young children to support, and a job change might entail a major adjustment.

The coordinator's performance did not improve much. Even though assistance was provided regarding program development and coordination procedures, and some improvements were made, it appeared that working relationships had been sufficiently damaged during several years and such a negative image had been established that satisfactory improvements were not likely. A book on supervising and terminating unsatisfactory employees contained some suggestions that the director found useful.

The coordinator was given notice of termination, due-process procedures were followed, and she appealed. Because both the associate director and the director had participated in the process, the dean of instruction to whom the director reported reviewed the case. The appeal was denied. The director and the coordinator were sufficiently close that they discussed the coordinator's career directions and the director helped her relocate to a similar position elsewhere where she could apply what she had learned in a new setting. As the director and associate director searched for and selected a new coordinator, they reviewed the match between the position and the applicants in an effort to reduce structural problems and achieve a satisfactory fit.

This example illustrates some of the ways in which interpersonal relations are important in staffing decisions. Forces in the community and in the college were interacting with the coordinator's approach and resulted in damage to her performance and to her ability to win and maintain cooperation. The director was more able to recognize these relationships than was the coordinator and by the time she did recognize them, most of the damage was done. Technical procedures were also relevant. The coordinator's inadequate use of program development and coordination procedures left some of the people with whom she worked questioning the value of her contribution. The director's effective use of due-process procedures and confirming memos may have avoided misunderstandings and disputes in a situation rife with conflict and angry feelings. But the crucial proficiency of the director and associate director in this instance was their effective practice of human relations.

Working with staff members, especially over a complex and trying issue, calls for considerable self-understanding and consideration for others. The attitudinal and ethical aspects of decision making regarding such staffing issues entail attention to the needs, aspirations, and beliefs of all parties concerned. High motivation, morale, and productivity are among the results of attention to human relations aspects of decision making.

At least two types of conflict are pertinent to the foregoing example. One was the conflict between the coordinator and some of the people with whom she dealt in the college and in the community. A second was the conflict between the coordinator, who wanted to continue, and the people to whom she reported, who eventually decided on termination. Effective decision making in this instance might include attention both to helping the coordinator (or her successor) deal with interpersonal and role conflict and to handling the process of performance review in ways that minimize destructive conflict.

The administration of continuing education is very susceptible to conflict because administrators are involved in so many goals and domains. Conflict is likely to surface when people associated with an agency have incompatible claims on the agency. Typical conflict situations are a personal feud between two members, a struggle between two ideological factions, alleged persecution of a staff member by a superior, conflicts regarding priorities, and a breakdown of cooperation between two departments (Caplow, 1976).

Effective decision-making strategies for reducing conflict depend on the type of conflict. For example, conflicts about priorities usually reflect differing values, aspirations, and beliefs that are difficult to analyze and resolve. Although it is well to start by exploring differing viewpoints and rationales and perhaps discovering misunderstandings, it is likely that an administrator will have to settle for bringing the antagonists together, seeking areas of agreement, and working out acceptable compromises. However, if a breakdown of cooperation between two related departments reflects a boundary dispute over a function both claim (such as selection of resource persons, deciding to cancel an activity due to low enrollment, or access to income beyond direct costs), a specific compromise is less likely to be effective than a clarification of boundaries or role expectations. Ways to do so include the implementation of policy changes and the creation of administrative teams.

When the conflict is among departments of the continuing education division, the director can deal with the problem directly. However, when the conflict is between the division and the departments of the parent organization, the problem can be more difficult and administrators in other parts of the parent organization (such as the person to whom the director reports) may have to help if the conflict is to be resolved. In such circumstances, a policy change may be a necessary ingredient in improved decision making.

In addition to effective decision-making strategies for conflict resolution, it should be recognized that commitment to shared goals and respect for others can help enable staff members to deal with the pressures that are part of any organization, to avoid the path to destructive conflict, and to use procedures for conflict resolution. While destructive conflict is a liability, creative tension from healthy differences is an asset.

Selection

Fortunately, most staffing decisions in continuing education entail little conflict. Those who help adults learn or who coordinate such programs typically welcome an opportunity to be associated with the agency and want to perform effectively. Sometimes a decision to hire a staff member may be influenced by standard procedures in the parent organization (Schneider, 1976).

The work of a continuing education agency can be performed by staff members employed by the agency or by people outside the agency who are hired on a contract basis. The decision about which arrangement to use can be a perplexing one for an administrator, especially when he or she is new to the parent organization.

Several years ago, an experienced manager of education and training moved to a larger division of his company after having directed the staff and organization department of a sister organization. For his former organization, the manager supervised a large and able staff that designed and also conducted most of the education and training activities for employees. The new division hired him because they wanted him to build a strong education department.

From his past experience, the manager believed that the most efficient way to do so would be to hire the necessary staff for his department both to design programs and deliver them. He recommended this policy to the director of human resource development, to whom he reported. The director disagreed.

The director felt, from his longer experience with the division, that it was very difficult to add personnel to the departmental payroll, but it was much easier to add money. Given the two main alternatives of employing or contracting, it might be more efficient to hire, but it would be easier to obtain a larger budget for contract services than to hire permanent staff.

The manager readily agreed. It was clear that the question did not involve the most efficient staffing arrangement for companies in general, but the best organizational strategy to achieve departmental objectives in this specific instance. The director and manager thus recommended to the vice-president for personnel a budget for the department that would enable the manager to hire a small staff to develop programs and to contract with people to conduct educational activities. As the effectiveness of department programs was recognized, full-time department staff members could be employed to deliver programs—if the idea could be sold to senior managers. Sometimes a short-term, less cost-effective strategy may be necessary until a department's performance warrants a demand to obtain a long-term and most cost-effective approach.

More typically, continuing education administrators select and orient people who will work for the agency on a full-time or part-time basis. Most full-time agency staff members are in administrative, supervisory, or support staff roles. Most people who teach adults on behalf of continuing education agencies do so on a part-time or short-term basis.

Because it entails fairly major long-term commitments, decision making to recruit, select, and orient full-time continuing education staff tends to be fairly formal (Knox and Associates, 1980, chap. 7). Decisions cluster around justifying the position; preparing the position description and job specifications; publicizing the position; and then searching for, screening, and selecting applicants for the position. Subsequent decisions are related to orientation, supervision, and staff and organization development activities to help assure the success of the person selected. In large organizations, the personnel department can help with parts of the process. In addition, guidelines from the personnel administration field generally (and affirmative action procedures in particular) can help an administrator move through a series of decisions that are satisfactory for the parent organization, the persons interested in the position, and especially the agency that depends on the effectiveness of such personnel decisions for its success.

By contrast, decison making for part-time staff (which includes most of the people who actually teach adults) is quite informal. Typically, those involved in the decision-making process include a program administrator, perhaps a planning or advisory committee, and sometimes people from the parent organization. Although the decision may seem quite personal, if the process is effective it is rarely solitary (Brown and Copeland, 1979).

Most continuing education agencies accumulate a cadre of people who have taught adults successfully for that agency before. These successful performers are very important to program administrators for several reasons, including reducing the burden of having to recruit and select new teachers each time, being predictably effective based on past performance with the agency, and having a following that helps attract participants. The cadre grows as those who have performed well are invited to do so again and those who have not are not offered another opportunity. Like talent scouts, the most able program administrators tend to be constantly on the lookout for promising resource persons and encourage them to contribute as a way of enriching the talent pool from which to select. In some instances, very attractive resource persons are asked to suggest new activities, then other program development decisions follow that basic staffing decision.

Members of planning and advisory committees and continuing education administrators from other providers can help enormously in the process of identifying potential resource persons, obtaining first-hand assessments of how well they perform and under what circumstances, and encouraging those selected to agree to teach. For agencies in higher education institutions, one source of resource persons is the full-time faculty of the college or university. In this instance, for staffing evening or off-campus credit courses, a department chair or division director or dean from the parent organization is likely to be part of the decision-making process. These parent organization administrators can be very committed to and supportive of the continuing education function of the institution, and they can be a major asset and ally for the continuing education administrator. Less supportive deans and department chairs can have quite different priorities that confound the continuing education staffing process and shift decision-making concerns toward conflict resolution (Daigneault, 1963). Similarly, company managers can either help or hinder staffing activities of the education and training department.

All of the people who help recruit and select teachers of adults (program administrators, planning committee members, deans) use incentives to do so. Some incentives, such as honoraria, are tangible and explicit. Many are not, such as visibility for referrals that specialists in a professional field may receive or recognition that may improve chances for a promotion. There are sometimes disincentives, such as negative attitudes toward outreach activities that can appear during faculty promotion or tenure decisions in research-oriented universities. Decision-making strategies for staffing should thus consider the role to be performed, encouraging the most able people to apply (given the available incentives), and organizational influences on the recruitment and selection process (Votruba, 1981).

Development

One paradox of continuing education practice is that the professed commitment to continuing education for program participants is so little matched by continuing education opportunities for the staff members who plan and conduct the programs. Moderately high staff turnover rates and the ease with which unsatisfactory performers can be removed contribute to this oversight. High turnover reflects the responsiveness of most parts of the field to participant satisfaction and to fluctuations in funding levels, along with a tendency for staff members who are very successful to go on to bigger and better opportunities and for those who are not successful to go on to other activities. The rewards are great for those who produce results.

The neglect of staff development for continuing education administrators and resource persons is especially severe for people who are new to the field and in need of orientation. Most people who enter the field do so without specialized preparation to help adults learn or to coordinate educational programs for adults. Many bring with them valuable backgrounds from related fields and in a few years some learn much of what they need to know. The difficulty with this "sink or swim" approach is that program quality can be low while newcomers are learning the ropes, and people with real promise become discouraged and leave the field. Orientation of new staff could reduce these problems (Spear, 1976).

Staff development for new or experienced continuing education resource persons and administrators contains some distinctive features to be taken into account. These features include the following.

1. Many staff members are part-time and work at scattered times and locations, which makes it difficult to assemble many at a time and place for staff development activities.
2. Staff members have exceedingly varied backgrounds, which makes it difficult to serve many well with any one activity.
3. Transiency and turnover of those who plan and conduct continuing education activities discourages much investment in staff development.
4. Marginality and instability of many agencies due to fluctuations in funding and staff inadequacies undermine an easy allocation of time and resources to staff development.
5. There is a widespread belief that effective continuing education consists mainly of effective interpersonal relations and common sense, and little exists by way of a knowledge base to strengthen and guide those involved. This discourages attention to staff development.

Fortunately, there are a number of assets that can just about compensate for those liabilities. Some of the major ones are:

1. Many of the people who work in continuing education do so in part because of a strong belief that lifelong learning is both desirable and feasible.
2. There is general recognition that improved staff performance can benefit participants, so it can be justified as an agency expense.
3. Many staff members are expert in procedures to help adults learn, and their knowledge could be used for their own benefit.
4. The educational backgrounds of staff members are sufficient for the use of self-directed learning activities if they are interested.
5. Some members of the field realize that a substantial amount of knowledge about adult learning, teaching, program development, and administration has accumulated in recent years, the dissemination of which could improve practice.

Decision-making strategies for the orientation and development of continuing education teachers and administrators should take such features into account, but consideration of background information does not add up to a strategy. Listed below are some action steps that can be adapted by a continuing education director to fit local circumstances.

1. Use the same sound procedures and arrangements for educational activities for agency staff as would be used for agency participants. Involve them in the process so that the benefits of improved agency functioning justify the costs of time and resources.

2. Review current activities that contribute to staff orientation and development, then make modest changes to prune and add to strengthen at the points most likely to produce improvements. Ask staff members what helped them most and least to develop and what they would prefer in the future. Obtain outside assistance, if needed.

3. Find out about the professional literature that seems best suited to

help plan and conduct staff development activities in your situation. For example, an overview of the proficiencies of continuing education practitioners (Knox, 1979) may help a staff development committee identify likely topics of interest among staff members that could be confirmed by a staff meeting or a brief checklist. An overview of generalizations about adult development and learning (Knox, 1977) might contain some excerpts for prior reading for a staff development session. A pamphlet on teaching adults (Bock, 1979) might be sent to all new instructors and loan copies of an overview on teaching adults effectively (Knox, 1980a) made available for both instructors and program administrators. Basic ideas about program development (Houle, 1972; Knowles, 1980) might be called to the attention of inexperienced program administrators, along with an overview of program development and administration (Knox and Associates, 1980). Readings on needs assessment (Pennington, 1980) or working with part-time teachers (Brown and Copeland, 1979), or reaching hard-to-reach adults (Darkenwald and Larson, 1980) could be available in the agency and called to the attention of staff members interested in improving those aspects of their practice.

4. Recognize that many practitioners learn and change more from interaction with more able peers than they do from reading. Reading a set of excerpts may be a vehicle for discussion with other staff members who become part of colleague networks that benefit some of the most able practitioners in the field. Courses and association meetings that establish contact with counterparts in other agencies and other locations can be especially valuable.

5. Include a range of learning activities that accommodate interests, circumstances, and the preferred learning styles of staff members. Their expertise in continuing education can contribute to sound selection. Their exposure to a wider range of activities could enrich the methods they use as practitioners to the benefit of agency participants. In addition to the many types of temporary groups such as courses and workshops, consider procedures for self-directed learning (Knowles, 1975; Knox, 1974) and for organizational development (Lindquist, 1978; Schein, 1978). Schein also presents a very useful rationale for attending to both individual and organizational needs in staff development activities.

6. Allocate some staff time and agency resources for staff development, designate someone to coordinate it, and support and reward successful efforts. Remember that a distinctive contribution of an agency director is decision making about the decision making process. Help staff members make decisions to improve staff development. They may improve their decision making in other domains as well. Teaching and learning are hopelessly and hopefully entwined and, like a rope, lose their strength when disentwined.

Supervision

Continuing education agencies tend to be results-oriented because responsive and effective programs acquire resources and those that are not successful tend to lose them. Optimism and a commitment regarding lifelong learning permeate participants, resource persons, administrators, and support staff. Many resource persons are experts in their fields with a habit of deciding what they will do and how. Most continuing education agencies are dependent units of parent organizations that can greatly influence how the agency functions. These characteristics have far-reaching implications for decision-making strategies related to the supervision of continuing education staff members.

Concepts of Supervision. Some aspects of effective supervision apply to most situations, including working with continuing education staff. Supervision is mainly concerned with producing results. Effective achievement of goals is the first consideration, followed by the efficient use of resources to do so. In practice, concern for production and concern for people are interconnected in both work situations and administrative style (Blake and Mouton, 1964). Much advice about organizational leadership boils down to winning agreement on important organizational goals that relate to member aspirations, encouraging them to contribute to goal achievement, and treating them fairly.

Much writing about supervision assumes that supervisors have more power in the organization than the people they supervise, and that supervisors directly control the work of those they oversee. Guidelines for direct supervision include focusing on the work instead of the person doing it, setting clear goals and emphasizing organizational priorities, encouraging and giving credit for accomplishment, building teamwork, emphasizing essential roles, and retaining final authority. For most continuing education administrators such guidelines are not sufficient. Because staff members (and especially instructors) have much expertise and independence, the following guidelines for indirect supervision are suggested.

1. Establish effective working relationships and jointly develop objectives, plans, and projections against which to evaluate performance.
2. Concentrate on important attainable goals and respect successful programs.
3. Recognize fiscal controls as an important source of supervisory leverage.
4. Be familiar with the program. With the emphasis of indirect supervision on productivity and results instead of the use of standard procedures, a premium is placed on criteria the supervisor can use to assess effectiveness. Aside from enrollments, cost recovery, and a positive image, several agency characteristics reflect high productivity. They include general agreement within the organization about what constitutes productivity, outstanding performance by an individual or group (which tends to be its own reward), people throughout the agency who are committed to high-quality performance, problems solved by staff members without administrative intervention, and the imitation of the agency by other providers more than it imitates them (Caplow, 1976).

Motivation to Grow. As talent managers, effective supervisors of teachers of adults seek not only to recognize high-quality continuing education but also to work with the experts who conduct continuing education activities to help them improve program quality. Decisions about how best to do so can be enhanced by attention to a sense of proficiency and esteem. A basic need and source of motivation is to maintain and enhance the sense of self-worth. Esteem is a powerful motivator of performance; it encourages people to increase and test their proficiency, which in turn can enhance self-esteem.

Needs that are on a lower level than self-esteem (such as affiliation and security) are associated with sources of work dissatisfaction such as salary, working conditions, and supervision. Needs that are on a higher level than self-esteem (such as autonomy and self-actualization) are associated with sources of work satisfaction from the work process and from achievement (Herzberg, 1966; Maslow, 1954; Sergiovanni and Carver, 1980). Although some workers seem to be mainly motivated by low-level needs and seek to avoid failure, most teachers of adults do so to meet higher-level needs and seek success. To be sure, they can be discouraged by poor salary, supervision, benefits, working conditions, and interpersonal relations. Supervisory attention to these externals is likely to reduce some sources of dissatisfaction but will contribute little to satisfaction and motivation. High-quality work performance and motivation are more likely to result from attention to meaningful work, responsibility for outcomes, and knowledge of outcomes. Thus effective decision-making strategies for supervision emphasize working with agency staff members so that members engage in varied and important tasks, have responsibility for producing results, and receive feedback regarding their performance (Hackman, Lawler, and Porter, 1977).

An important aspect of supervision is teaching in the best sense. Dynamics of the teaching-learning relationship are accepted when making decisions about the interaction between resource persons and participants. This relationship is less often considered as central to effective interactions between supervisor and teacher, but it should be. Levinson (1968) makes a powerful case for a two-way teacher-learner dialogue as the core of effective supervision. This can be illustrated by consideration of relations between an agency director and a program coordinator whose work the director supervises.

Among expectations the coordinator might have of the director are encouragement, respect, consideration, and recognition. A director can help the coordinator take on and accomplish challenging and growthful tasks. A director who respects his or her coordinator does not exploit the coordinator for his or her own gain. An effective director looks out for the coordinator's interests and corrects the coordinator justly and in private. An effective director also gives credit for a successful performance. Such expectations are most likely to be met under conditions of mutual respect. Coordinators want to respect directors as people and as supervisors from whom they can learn. The mentor relationship that has been popularized in recent years illustrates this mutually beneficial situation when it is working well. The mentor relationship also illustrates the strains inherent in supervision. Such a relationship can easily accumulate frustrations, resentments, and general organizational tensions. A continuing constructive relationship usually requires that both parties work at it.

There are various ways for a director to encourage experienced coordinators to grow, that in concert can contribute to the achievement of both coordinators and agency goals. Some of them are listed below.

1. Encourage coordinators to assume challenging tasks under supportive conditions. Performance appraisal may provide an opportunity for mutual goal setting. In addition to shared expectations, support, and respect, the director should allow coordinators substantial freedom.

2. Inexperienced coordinators are doing more than accomplishing tasks; they are testing reality and exercising self-control. In the process, freedom and responsibility interact. Coordinator's responsibilities for outcomes and actions depend upon the freedom to act but also help coordinators discover limits to freedom and areas of freedom that are especially important to success. Acquiring and applying knowledge in action settings helps coordinators acquire a sense of proficiency that affects the tasks they undertake in the future.

3. Recognize that coordination, interpersonal relations, and decision making are interconnected. The best way to learn them all is in the work setting. Individual initiative and identification with a supervisor or mentor also contribute. The most powerful way in which a director can help coordinators grow is by building an organizational context that contains role models, encouragement to try, opportunities to practice, and constructive feedback. Such a supervisory approach is likely to produce better decisions and better coordinators.

Reorganization

Much of the foregoing discussion regarding staffing has focused on fairly specific choices affecting only a few people. In contrast, some staffing decisions (such as a major reorganization) affect many people and call for decision-making strategies that fit this purpose.

When the director of the public school continuing education division of a state education department was appointed, it appeared that some reorganization of the three bureaus was needed. Due to shifting support and staff attrition, only two of the bureaus were functioning and one of them was ten times as large as the other. Furthermore, the central office of the education department had reduced the budget of the small bureau; technical assistance to local districts was provided by both bureaus; the separate activities that reflected categorical funding encouraged discontinuity across adult basic education, high school completion, and general adult education at the local level; and occupational upgrading was not related to any of them.

As soon as the director understood the basic organizational problem, he prepared a list of specific problems that might be reduced through reorganization. The divisional staff reviewed the list and agreed with his suggestions. This helped achieve consensus on the nature of the problem. The director, who did not perceive himself as a specialist in organizational arrangements, asked a staff member to do some library research and prepare a proposal for the reorganization of the division.

The proposal reflected some desirable features of the technical assistance to be provided to local public school continuing education programs such as helping with long-range planning and reducing barriers associated with sources of funding or reporting requirements. The main recommendation was to organize the division into two bureaus. One would deal with field relationships and be composed of staff members who would work with local districts in each region of the state. The other would deal with program assistance and be composed of staff members who would identify new trends and developments to improve practice and respond to field staff requests for assistance.

The proposed reorganization was then described in a bulletin sent to all the local public school continuing education programs in the state for their reactions and suggestions, which were supportive. Positive reactions were also obtained from the assistant commissioner to whom the director reported.

At a division staff meeting to discuss the proposed reorganization, a few preferred not reorganizing, largely on the grounds that if bureaus remained along the lines of categorical aid it would be unnecessary to prorate staff time across several sources of support (which was part of the proposed reorganization plan). However, the majority of the staff supported the director's proposed reorganization. To complicate matters a bit, the decision was made outside the division to add a third bureau on occupational upgrading.

The director then sent a memo to his staff that described the modified reorganization plan on which he had decided. This plan was then sent to the education department and the civil service department for review and approval, which took a year. The director then sent a memo to his divisional staff and to practitioners in the field announcing the reorganization. He then asked each of his staff members for their preferences for assignments under the reorganization, and when all assignments were made, only two members were disappointed.

The director mentioned several concepts that were reflected in his approach to decision making. He saw his role as going beyond consensus and as including the building of support for desirable directions. His openness to staff expertise was reflected in his request that a staff member study and suggest some organizational arrangements when this was not a personal strength. The director's involvement of the assistant commissioner to whom he reported reflected an effort to obtain both useful ideas and support for implementation.

Concepts that also relate to criteria for judging satisfactory organizational arrangements are avoidance of organizational categories that restrict program development and the importance of satisfactory relations with associated organizations. This enables an administrator to orchestrate the flow of resources to support an agency and in other ways to facilitate system functioning. The administrator also believes that it is important to limit the number of initiatives and new activities so that there is sufficient time and resources to properly support those that are under way.

Part of the success of this reorganization stemmed from the attention the director gave to many aspects of the adjustment. As Lindquist (1978) has emphasized for faculty development, there are many forces that contribute to organizational inertia, and they should be addressed as part of a planned change strategy.

One source of useful information for someone trying to guide a major reorganization is an overview of the entire agency as a social system. A new director may have an advantage in making changes while an agency is involved in a transition and before new sources of inertia are solidified. However, it may take time for a new director to become sufficiently familiar with an agency and parent organization to provide effective leadership for the transition. An understanding of analyses of the agency or similar ones may accelerate the process of acquiring that familiarity. For example, if reorganization of an urban adult basic education program is being considered, reading a recent external review and *Last Gamble on Education* (Mezirow, Darkenwald, and Knox, 1975) might help a local director propose an organizational plan that addresses important features of the local situation.

When an administrator has a long association with an organization, an effective decision-making strategy is likely to reflect this. Such a strategy is illustrated by the following decision to broaden coordination of the outreach and continuing education function of a university.

The outreach, continuing education, and public service function of many universities have undergone some reorganization in recent years. A frequent issue in such reorganization has been the extent of institution-wide coordination of the outreach function. There are, of course, many specific decisions that are part of a global reorganization decision.

A major university recently underwent such a reorganization. For several decades, the director of continuing education coordinated many of the noncredit continuing education activities, and the dean of outreach coordinated another major portion of outreach activities. The remainder were scattered among many academic units. The two major portions were largely independent. The director was left alone to administer his division, and the dean of outreach administered his portion.

More than a decade ago, the director concluded that greater coordination of the total outreach function would be desirable but it was not a good time to raise the question. It seemed better to strengthen the educational and fiscal aspects of the division, establish strong relationships throughout the university, and gain experience and visibility.

A few years later the president arranged for a prominent expert in continuing education to study the university's outreach structure and function.

The expert recommended ways to strengthen and consolidate the outreach function. The report was shelved by the administration and no action was taken at that time. However, the director agreed with the recommendations, referred to them when appropriate, and used them as part of his long-term plan.

Some years later, the university experienced a change of president and of outlook regarding outreach. The director concluded that the time seemed right to raise the question of coordination of outreach. The division was in good shape internally and was well regarded in the university. It was currently enjoying two major external grants to support innovative continuing education activities, and a proposal for a third was in progress. A difficulty that had been identified in relation to several of these externally supported projects was the lack of adequate coordination of outreach. When several new administrators asked the director about how outreach might be strengthened, he mentioned the coordination difficulty (especially in relation to the proposal in process) and made some suggestions (based on the earlier expert's report).

Several developments in the division in the preceding few years helped pave the way for a reorganization decision. The governance and committee structure of the division had not been restricted to internal matters but included attention to and representation of university-wide outreach activities. This was reflected in the program development committee of the division and in an informal network of coordinators of independent continuing education activities throughout the university. They had started to publish a listing of outreach activities from various parts of the institution. The division was providing continuing education marketing services for other units.

As a way of encouraging the president to appoint a faculty committee to consider reorganization of outreach, the director suggested that the proposal that was in process was more likely to be funded if such a faculty committee were appointed. During the year in which a well-constituted committee was active it reviewed reports on outreach activities, read the earlier expert's report, talked with people engaged in outreach (including the director), and considered some alternative courses of action. The main recommendation in the committee report reflected the earlier expert's report that proposed all outreach activities be covered by one administrative structure and have one statutory faculty council. There was little committee support for the alternative that administrative arrangements for outreach be eliminated altogether at the university level. Greater coordination of outreach was generally seen as desirable. The dean of outreach, to whom the director reported, recommended that administrative arrangements remain as they were. This was rejected and he resigned. The faculty committee report and recommendations were approved by the executive committee of the senate and by the university council and are on their way to being implemented.

The process by which this series of decisions related to coordination of outreach was made reflect several influences beyond the weighing of evidence and alternatives at each decision point. Included are timing, perceptions of administrators and organizational divisions, and the broad base of support for the faculty committee recommendations that contained anticipated benefits for many people interested in outreach.

The director mentioned that some of the writings that he had found most helpful regarding decision making were classic texts on making judgments and on acquiring and using resources and support to achieve organizational goals and change.

Summary and Conclusions

As the foregoing examples on reorganization of the division and on coordination of outreach illustrate, a major agency reorganization can highlight many decisional issues related to staffing. Concerns about productivity can give rise to a reorganization and people affected by it can become so dissatisfied that they resign, as was the case in the previous example. The main themes of productivity and satisfaction recur in writings about organizational behavior, administrative style, small group behavior, and personality theory. Effective staffing decisions are likely to take both productivity and satisfaction into account.

One source of dissatisfaction for administrators themselves is conflict. Conflict is probably inevitable, especially in large organizations. Effective decisions about staffing consider the influence of existing conflict and likely conflicts associated with the alternative courses of action being considered. It is clearly dysfunctional to create unnecessary conflict. However, differences of goals, style, and opinion can contribute to creative tension within an organization that can lead to innovation and offset stagnation. The fairness and trust associated with decision making can influence whether differences lead to destructive conflict or constructive innovation.

Supervisory practices can also weigh in this balance. Many of the resource persons with whom program administrators work are talented experts who are quite powerful in their own fields. Some of these resource persons confront many time demands and program administrators want to convince them to devote some of their time to helping adults learn. Administrators are more likely to succeed in this process if they understand and use multiple incentives. For both resource persons and agency coordinators, effective administrators use a combination of indirect supervision, leading, and informal teaching in which one objective (and an evidence of the success of the supervisory relationship) is personal growth by individual staff members. In short, decision making by effective program administrators is more similar to that by talent managers than top sergeants.

Program administrators both select staff and help decide on tasks that resource persons and coordinators will perform. This means that decisional strategies should include attention to matching of people and roles. In some cases job assignments are within the agency, as in the case of conference coordinators. However, in some cases decision making includes people from the parent organization, as in the case of selecting full-time university faculty members to teach evening or off-campus credit courses for adults. In the latter situation, efforts to improve the staffing process may entail procedures for organizational change. In either case, a number of people are likely to be involved in this process. This chapter also emphasizes sources for further reading that can enhance decision making regarding staffing.

Agency administrators confront multiple power centers in the agency, parent organization, and service area that call for diplomacy in dealing with conflicting values.

External Relations

Most of the decision making with which continuing education administrators are associated occurs within the agency. Some of the decisions are fairly technical, such as those that relate to accounting, marketing, or equipment. Some decisions mainly involve human relations, such as resolving a dispute among several staff members. However, some of the decisions that are most influential on agency functioning deal mainly with external relations and are influenced greatly by people outside the agency. This chapter includes generalizations and examples on making decisions that pertain to relations with the parent organization, other providers, and the larger society.

Because decisions on external relations pertain to and are influenced by people outside the agency who may lack familiarity with and commitment to agency goals and activities, it is important that agency administrators have a broad perspective on the context in which the agency functions and on leadership strategies likely to be effective in that context. Therefore, as a background for dealing with specific external relations decisions, it would be helpful for an inexperienced administrator to become familiar with basic generalizations about ways in which organizations interact with their environment (Katz and Kahn, 1978), ways in which agencies can strengthen relations with their parent organizations (Votruba, 1981), ways of providing administrative leadership (Knox and Associates, 1980).

When actually participating in decision making regarding external relations issues, effective administrators may use concepts and procedures from all aspects of leadership, but the emphasis is likely to reflect the external focus of the issues. Typically, when moving from internal to external decisions, the emphasis shifts from scientific to artistic insights and from organizational to political dynamics. Beliefs and values become even more central.

Interpersonal relations with external people associated with decision making shifts from their being recipients of planning or evaluation conclusions to their being influencers of the process and of the ways in which conclusions are used. The lack of long-range planning for continuing education agencies reflects many influences, including pluralistic providers, agency marginality, commitment to responsiveness, and fluctuations in support. One way to strengthen planning is for agency administrators to use decision-making strategies that effectively involve people from the parent organization, other providers, regulatory organizations, and the larger society.

Influences on Priorities

Priorities for continuing education are seldom set in a policy statement, such as legislation, and then implemented. More often they simply evolve. Continuing education administrators who have a sense of direction and who are able to work effectively with key people in the parent organization can use program successes to help policy makers in the parent organization recognize and agree to priorities for continuing education. The following example shows how this can occur gradually, with leadership provided by someone who began as a volunteer and then worked as an entry-level staff member and proceeded to guide the emergence of a continuing education division.

Many educational programs for adults evolve gradually as a result of a series of decisions that are far more clear in retrospect. The coordinator of the continuing education division of a major natural history museum reflected on how her division emerged during the past six years and how some of the key decisions came about.

In the mid-seventies, the education department was undergoing some reorganization. As part of larger trends and adjustments related to finance and personnel policies in the total museum, there was a freeze on staffing and a reconsideration of the goals of the education department. The department had dealt mainly with school groups and had done little for adults from the general public.

The coordinator had started with the museum as a volunteer. She was asked to help on a paid basis after two staff members in the education department left and there was a change in chairperson. The coordinator worked with one of the few educational activities for adults in the museum at that time, which was a volunteer program supported by a grant from the National Endowment for the Arts.

It seemed to her that in addition to the benefits it provided for the museum and its visitors, volunteer activity could provide valuable educational experiences for the volunteers themselves. She herself had learned much from working with volunteers and museum personnel while supervising a grant-supported project. The volunteer effort grew and established a positive image in and for the museum.

During that period, the Department of Education received funding for continuing education activities related to an exhibit on environmental issues. This provided an opportunity to explore some of the additional types of educational activities for adults that the department might provide. People connected with the department were aware of the many, varied, and expanding continuing education offerings by higher education institutions and other providers in the region. The department offered various educational activities for adults and concluded that they should restrict themselves to what they did best and not attempt what other providers could do better. The decision was made that all continuing education activities for the general public should be exhibit-related. The only activities that were retained that did not involve the exhibit on environmental issues were some environmental field trips and a prominent lecture series. This exploration of future directions for continuing education by the museum entailed consideration of the priorities of museum staff and trustees, who tended to be reluctant to move in new directions.

During that first year or two, the coordinator became part of a core group to prepare grant proposals to obtain external support for innovative programs. When a promising program idea was identified and before she would draft a proposal, the coordinator would discuss the idea in detail with a curator or someone else likely to implement the program if it was funded and would find out what other providers were doing along those lines. After a proposal was drafted, she would continue to discuss it in order to refine the plan and maintain momentum. After the proposal was funded and the program was operating, museum staff and trustees and others raised questions that led to refinements, policy decisions, and ideas for future programs.

Between the grant-supported activities, film and lecture series, and self-sustaining courses, the continuing education effort expanded rapidly. In the first five years, the courses for adults expanded from five classes with less than 150 total enrollment to fifty courses and more than 1,500 total enrollment. In two more years, the number of courses doubled. As the continuing education division expanded, staff was added and the coordinator hired an assistant.

For each major expansion, proposal, or change, the decision-making process was fairly similar. The coordinator took the leadership for program development but involved many other people in the process. When a proposal began to emerge it was discussed with the chairperson of the department of education, with the assistant director for science and education, and with the members of the program planning and evaluation committee of the board of trustees (which included some staff representation). At each step in the process, the plan could be modified and a go/no-go decision could be made. In addition to specific program details, the coordinator attended to the global concerns that staff and trustees had about the desirability and riskiness of a proposed project, and she tried to use such opportunities to explain the rationale, identify the benefits, and to provide general reassurance.

Although alternatives were discussed in relation to decisions about individual courses and proposals, alternatives were not explicitly discussed in relation to the general evolution of the division over a period of six years. It was more a matter of gradually achieving consensus about the desirability of a continuing education mission for the museum and about the feasibility of doing so. The coordinator believes that the more the division does, the better it does it as it gains in experience, staff, visibility, expertise, and commitment. She recognizes that her experience with and reading about volunteerism has been an asset. Winning and maintaining cooperation has been an essential ingredient. Another essential has been a sense of direction, a receptivity to surroundings and trends in the larger community outside the museum that helps museum staff and trustees recognize ways in which they can be responsive to educational needs of adults in their region.

In the process of gradual and informal decision making to create a new program, an important part of the strategy was to build commitment to continuing education among policy makers in the museum. That strategy included defining a distinctive mission of the museum in relation to other providers, balancing programs across museum specialties, and starting small and guiding growth as the program evolved.

In contrast, the next example discusses an administrator who confronted many continuing education providers and activities for members of a professional association. The administrator's task was to define a distinctive contribution for the association on behalf of the total continuing effort in the professional field.

As does any other provider of continuing education, professional associations define their educational mission. The parameters of this mission are created by the choices that are made, regardless of how deliberately alternatives are considered. Some national associations decide to become major providers of educational programs for their members, but there are other roles that can be assumed. One professional association has charted a distinctive course for its continuing education mission.

Ten years ago the association decided to develop procedures to ensure the continued competency of practitioners in the field. A task force recommended that standards of practice be defined and that until they were and procedures were established for examination and peer review based on those standards, continuing education was encouraged as a way of promoting continued competence. However, the association rejected continuing education participation as evidence of competence.

The appointment of the director of education for the association during this period took into account the background and interests of the person selected as well as the general stance and specific policies of the association regarding continuing education. After the appointment the director and the two major policy groups of the association worked together closely, and each influenced the other as decisions were made regarding the continuing education mission. A general belief that pervaded these decisions was that, although the association had an important role regarding competence, it was mainly the responsibility of the individual practitioner to perform well.

The organization that accredits professional schools in the field set up a procedure for accreditation of providers of continuing education that included standards for judging continuing education. A national study was conducted to identify and gain agreement on standards of professional practice in the field. These standards were then used to create self-assessment exercises to enable practitioners to compare their knowledge and performance to the standards.

Throughout this process, the director of education helped clarify and implement the association's mission regarding continuing education. Two broad themes have been an unwavering commitment to continuing education as a means to maintain and increase competence but not an end in itself and a belief that agencies other than the association should act as major providers of continuing education. As a result, the director's role has been more concerned with linkage among organizations and resources than with coordination of continuing education activities.

In addition to working with the committees, task forces, and studies already referred to, the director's approach has included several types of activities. One has been giving talks and participating in committees and projects both in the field and in conjunction with other professional fields. This has helped to identify and test useful ideas with and from other fields as well as to build and maintain consensus within the association. Another activity has been working with various providers of continuing education, such as state associations, universities, and a journal published by the association. In working with these providers, the director tried to help them relate their efforts closer to professional competence and the process of problem solving. These efforts have included the preparation of handbooks on the use of local resources for learning, encouraging practitioners to work with local agencies that could identify problems that they could help solve, and negotiating with the editor of the journal for inclusion of articles that might serve as vehicles for continuing education.

Another example of the director's activities related to continuing eduation has been his participation in a major university project to develop practice audit procedures for continuing education needs assessment and program development. His role was to help develop and field test the procedures written in his own field before the university project staff proceeded to develop parallel procedures for other professional fields.

Several concepts were mentioned by the director regarding decisions he made about his role and the mission of the association in continuing education. One is the centrality of competency and performance in dealing with questions of accountability and professionalism. The main focus of competency occurs in the marketplace as practitioners make decisions and solve problems. Continuing education activities are useful to enhance competence but do not take the place of standards of performance. Thus, ideas about how learning activities can relate more closely to the details of professional practice have been of special interest. This reflects a broader concern about consumerism and accountability. It seems desirable for recipients of professional services to understand and be able to judge the quality of services provided by practitioners. Likewise, it seems desirable for professionals to participate in decisions regarding their own continuing education. Thus, in addition to writings on continuing professional education, the director has valued writings on assessing competence and experiential learning.

Authority and Influence

Although they worked in different settings (museum, association), and at different stages in the development of a large continuing education effort, each of these two administrators approached decision making in relation to the parent organization from a sense of their own authority. Administrative authority is the potential capacity to encourage people to help achieve goals (Sergiovanni and Carver, 1980). One major source of authority is the administrator's formal role, which is perceived in relation to the ability to help achieve goals and invoke sanctions (such as resource allocation and staffing decisions). A second major source of authority is the administrator's informal influence as a person, which is derived from both substantive expertise and interpersonal abilities and which emphasizes the satisfaction of his or her followers. As with most continuing education administrators, neither of these administrators had much formal authority from their role (especially at the outset, in the museum example). Each had to accumulate and use the sources of influence available to them to encourage others to embrace and help achieve goals important to continuing education. They had to perform this role in ways that fit the specific situation in which they worked.

Centralization and Decentralization

Another way to illustrate situational influences on leadership is to compare the general decision-making strategies of two continuing higher education administrators, one who directed a division in which most continuing education activities of the institution were administratively centralized and another who coordinated continuing education activities that were for the most part administratively decentralized in major academic units. In both instances academic decisions about program purposes, content, and some aspects of staffing were left to faculty members and other members of planning committees.

In the administratively centralized agency, the academic units gave little attention to continuing education programs, budgets, or faculty involvement. The central administration seemed satisfied with the slight involvement but appreciated the good public relations. The faculty enjoyed much autonomy and worked out arrangements directly with the division. The continuing education division staff handled many of the details of program development, finances, records, reports, program marketing, and incentives for faculty members and arrangements for external resource persons. Staff satisfaction came from working with clients. The clients may have had a more visible single door for continuing education activities and easier arrangements for multidisciplinary activities.

By contrast, in the administratively decentralized agency, the academic units typically devoted more attention and faculty effort to continuing education programs and arrangements but had some resistance to multidisciplinary activities. The central administration was more concerned about consistency of policies, use of internal resources, and avoiding problems related to outreach. Faculty members retained much of their autonomy, but related continuing education more closely to their other activities. Continuing education division staff worked with faculty and staff in academic units on program development, dealt with parent organization influences on division efforts, monitored scattered activities and expenditures to report on institutional efforts and to respond to inquiries from potential participants, and disseminated some public information on behalf of the total outreach effort. Clients experienced more difficulty locating scattered and compartmentalized activities, but may have experienced greater departmental commitment and continuity.

Table 2 compares highlights of leadership strategies that administrators might use in these two contrasting settings. Each item on the list is a task typically performed by a continuing higher education administrator who uses a general strategy consistent with each of the two settings. The tasks are grouped according to the major *activities* in which they engaged, the types of *policies* related to continuing education, the types of *influence* and responsibilities, and *leadership* to facilitate program development.

Leadership Roles

Most administrators inherit written and oral expectations of their role, often influenced by the performance of their predecessors. Influences that the history of the agency and organization can have on an administrator's role are illustrated by the following example of procedures to specify a role and gain agreement within the parent organization.

When an administrator is appointed to an established position, a general idea of the role and function and even a detailed position description reflect organizational expectations. However, when an administrator is the first incumbent of a newly created position, an early decision may be useful to obtain agreement on the administrator's role and function.

This process is illustrated by the experience of a newly appointed director of management and organization development for the corporate headquarters of a large company. Although the director had been with the company in another capacity for several years, she was the first incumbent in this position. A clarification of her role and function seemed especially important because there were changes in related staff positions around that time that affected expectations regarding her role. Also, the close association of several families

Table 2. Comparison of Leadership Strategies in Administratively Centralized and Decentralized Continuing Higher Education Divisions

Centralized	Decentralized
Activities	
1. Identifying promising program directions	1. Establishing linkage with potential clients and assisting with needs assessment
2. Separately conducting some noncredit activities	2. Encouraging faculty members to initiate programs
3. Working with continuing education specialists mainly in the division	3. Working with continuing education specialists mainly in the colleges
4. Arranging for facilities and support services	4. Coordinating scattered services
5. Administering program budgets	5. Monitoring scattered program budgets
Communication	
1. Communicating with current and potential clients	1. Facilitating contact between colleges and clients (counseling services) and institutional marketing
2. Encouraging mutual understanding among division staff	2. Arranging for interchange among colleges (council)
3. Reporting to central administration	3. Monitoring total continuing education effort (management information system)
Policies	
1. Administering division policies	1. Developing central administration and faculty support for institutional policies
2. Using comparable guidelines in dealing with individual professors	2. Encouraging colleges to support continuing education (faculty rewards)
3. Administering division financial arrangements	3. Developing collaborative financial arrangements
Influence	
1. Controlling own budgets and resource allocations	1. Influencing a wider range of resource allocation related to continuing education
2. Directly providing incentives and rewards to instructors	2. Influencing the basic academic reward structure as well

3. Building public support for division

4. Coordinating division services to clients

3. Building public support for the institution

4. Providing service to colleges

Leadership

1. Serving as a director with management responsibility

2. Having administrative expertise to conduct programs (except those that colleges want) with little direct participation in academic concerns

3. Selecting and working with professors as individuals

4. Identifying desirable direction for continuing education

1. Serving as an associate vice-president for academic affairs with indirect coordination responsibility

2. Having academic leadership regarding continuing education purposes and resources and encouraging colleges to deal with continuing education clients

3. Helping to develop commitment and capability of professors and administrators to conduct continuing education

4. Identifying desirable and likely directions for continuing education function as it relates to remainder of institution

---

with the company suggested that a brief review of the company's history would help in the preparation of a position description.

The newly appointed director decided to prepare a charter for her position as a basis for a position description. In doing so, she worked closely with the vice-president for personnel to whom she reported. They also consulted and obtained concurrence from the vice chairman of the board. She started by reviewing the history of the company, including the pattern of acquisitions, products marketed, the evolving corporate mission, and biographies of key leaders. This review was based on reading documents and interviewing ten top corporate officers. The interviews also helped develop a charter for her position that would be consistent with their perceptions of the current corporate mission.

A draft of the charter was then reviewed by the vice-president for personnel and by members of the strategic planning group. This review was especially helpful in obtaining suggestions about how her position, which was concerned with management and growth of employees, could be related to other aspects of planning and control. The vice-president for personnel presented a draft of the charter at a company-wide meeting of executives, it was discussed, and suggestions were sent to the vice-president for personnel. The vice-president for public affairs helped edit a draft.

It took about two months for the process of reviewing company history and preparing a charter for the new position so that it would be consistent with the corporate mission, including the suggestions from key executives and successive revisions. On the basis of the charter, a specific job description was prepared.

The decision to prepare the charter and the process that was used in part reflect writings by Harry Levinson (1968) and others that have emphasized the importance of understanding organizational dynamics as a basis for managerial effectiveness. In addition to achieving consensus among top management regarding a new role, the process resulted in visibility and a basis for future working relationships with others in top management. In retrospect the charter was a conceptual document, and managers tend to be pragmatic. Because too much time elapsed before the charter was made operational in the form of a job description and actual performance, some managers began to wonder why the charter was being prepared and what the director's position would be in practice. In this instance, the decision-making process emphasized achieving consensus on the function of a new director of management and organizational development in an effort not only to clarify the position but also to establish relationships that could help in the implementation of the plan.

Many administrators feel some ambivalence about their leadership role, especially when dealing with people in the parent organization or elsewhere who challenge assumptions about leading and following. Some insights by Levinson (1968) are especially helpful in dealing with feelings about administrative roles.

Leading and following are closely intertwined, as are teaching and learning in the best practice. Followers prefer leaders to help agree on and achieve desirable goals. Thus, effective leaders tend to be expert, consistent, and cosmopolitan. Because followers also dislike being submissive, effective leaders tend to be considerate and give attention to follower satisfaction. Leader power can result in too little attention to follower satisfaction in relation to task achievement. But especially in continuing education, leadership depends on the consent of followers. Administrators who have to resort very often to the use of power and sanctions associated with their role have probably lost most of their ability to lead. To win and maintain consent depends on understanding follower values and expectations. Because consent is temporary and leadership varies with the context (including followers), successful leaders maintain their integrity and psychological consistency but adapt the contribution that they and related leaders make as circumstances change. They also know that organizational performance and renewal depends on follower talents that they can release. Thus effective decision making includes the involvement of followers and attention to knowledge and attitudes so that all concerned learn better ways to solve problems. This creates sound decisions and enhanced staff proficiencies.

Administrators also have feelings about the leader role, including self-doubt, vulnerability, rivalry, and images of omnipotence. They realize that followers want consideration, recognition, and respect from leaders, but they also realize that followers have both positive and negative attitudes toward leaders. Thus it helps leaders to understand that no leader can be all things to all people. An administrator has obligations to participants, staff, policy makers, funders, and even counterpart providers. Each of these relationships constitutes a source of power as well as an obligation for service. The sense of being the person in the middle pervades administration.

In these respects and others, administrative leadership is part of an individual-organizational relationship. Effective decision making reflects this joint effort in which administrators try to maintain equilibrium, exert initiative, and mediate disputes. Ineffective administrators encourage power seeking and rivalry, misplace personnel, and apply pressure on people of inadequate ability. Effective administrators are flexible, high in need for achievement but low in need for power and are aware of self, participants, and staff.

Interagency Relations

Some decision making entails relations with other providers of continuing education. The next example illustrates strategies that take into account interagency relations. Circumstances often precipitate a change. In this example, the public school adult education program was transferred to and absorbed by the local community college. (It should be noted that in some states competition for funds and participants has made these two types of providers fierce competitors. Note also in the following example how the past association between the dean of continuing education and the superintendent of the community college system facilitated the transfer.)

The dean of continuing education had the experience of having his program transferred from a school district to the local community college. Because of reductions in the school district budget four years previously, the dean had faced the prospect of loss of school district support for his continuing education program, which was large, well known, and served many adults from adjoining districts. An attractive alternative was to have the community college assume responsibility for the continuing education staff and programs in order to augment its current outreach programs for adults.

A few years earlier the dean had gotten to know the chairman of his school board. The chairman was also a member of the adult education advisory council and was interested in and committed to the continuing education offerings. That chairman went on to become the superintendent of the public educational system in that region, which included the community colleges. The dean contacted his friend, who had become superintendent, and proposed that the continuing education program be transferred to one of the community colleges. The superintendent liked the idea and suggested that such a transfer be proposed to the local community college president. Such a proposal required the support of the president of the community college as well as administrators from the school system. The superintendent, therefore, held a luncheon meeting for the community college president and the dean in his former role as director of the high school continuing education program. They all agreed on the desirability of such a transfer and on a collaborative approach to achieving it.

The dean's approach to the transfer and the series of related decisions was evolutionary. As in earlier years, he preferred to introduce a practice or program and try it on a small scale, and if it was successful it would spread. There was agreement that it was desirable to continue to use facilities in the school district in which the dean once had worked. As a result, he and his staff were in the community college for a year before many faculty members and administrators began to realize the extent of the continuing education activities that were now associated with the college.

Given the success of this transfer and the new delivery system through the community college, the superintendent of the educational system, the president of the community college, and the dean of continuing education met to expand this effort to include programs related to other public school systems.

As a result, the dean met with high school principals and interested staff members of adjacent school districts. Most of the school districts with limited continuing education offerings were interested in such a transfer because it offered expanded educational programs for adults in their district with little or no expense to the school district. (However, people associated with one school district with a large continuing education program were not interested in such a transfer. They belived that they would lose more than they gained.) Then the principals of the interested school districts met with members of the community college administrative cabinet to explore what would be entailed in the proposed transfer.

The dean was designated to coordinate the newly transferred programs on behalf of the community college and to work with several program administrators who had been associated with the other high school continuing education programs. Together, these administrators planned programs, arranged for people to teach them, worked with the cooperating high school principals regarding use of their space to hold programs, and worked with community leaders in the cooperating school districts to facilitate needs assessment and encourage participation.

In recent years, the community college has been moving toward a one college concept in which the continuing education function is increasingly integrated into the college. Major decisions are made by the president and his cabinet. Continuing education finances are handled by the college business office and marketing by the public information office. The dean and his staff emphasize program development. As regular enrollments have declined, there has been increased interest in noncredit continuing education activities. Continuing education has become a more central concern of the president and his cabinet as they make plans for the future of the college.

The dean characterized his approach to decision making as evolutionary and interactive. He wanted to continue and strengthen the continuing education program he had worked with for more than a decade in the school district, if at all possible. He tried to realistically assess the resources and contacts he had to help him do so. As key decisions were made, such as the transfer of his public school program to the community college, the dean tried to reflect these new realities in his plan of action.

During his decade as the only continuing education administrator in his school district, the dean interacted with many people in the school and in the community, but with the exception of his secretary he had no one with whom to discuss his plans and progress. Interaction with other members of his professional associates helped broaden his perspective and establish a network of colleagues with whom he could test his ideas. When the prospect of a transfer of his program to the college arose, he discussed it with a colleague with extensive experience in continuing higher education. Now with four program administrators on his staff at the college, he has easy opportunities for collegial interaction within his agency, and this is reflected in his current approach to decision making.

Most relations with other providers entail not a process of merger but an ongoing cooperative or competitive relationship with independent agencies. Most instances of cooperation are between agencies of different types and sizes; they complement each other, which is useful for sustained cooperation. (Two very similar agencies usually want the same contributions and benefits, which makes collaboration difficult.) However, administrators from two quite different agencies may have difficulty understanding how the other agency functions, which can confound decision making regarding collaborative efforts. A helpful concept in this regard is boundary maintenance.

Organizations have boundaries to help members and nonmembers know where the organization begins and ends. Most parent organizations with which continuing education agencies are associated have quite distinct boundaries that indicate who is an employee, a student, a customer, or a policy maker. Sometimes an identification card or badge is used to make clear who is a member and entitled to organization benefits. These constitute the primary boundaries of an organization.

Secondary boundary maintenance also occurs through inside organizational containment (based on internal cohesiveness and control) and through outside permeability (based on extensiveness of contact by people outside the organization and susceptibility to outside influence). Continuing education agencies tend to have lower boundary maintenance and to be more permeable that most other parts of their parent organization (Katz and Kahn, 1978). This is reflected in the image of continuing education administrators with one foot in the parent organization and one foot in the community.

Agencies vary in the extent and ways in which their secondary boundaries are maintained, which, if they are quite different and misunderstood, can impede cooperation among agencies. The following examples illustrate some of the main secondary boundary profiles. An example of high internal containment but high external permeability is a tightly knit adult-services office of a YWCA that has open registration and is very responsive to requests. An example of high containment but low permeability is a private evening college with high community demand, entrance requirements, and independence from the parent organization. An example of low containment but high permeability is a library extension program open to any adult in the region, responsive to most requests, and with each librarian working independently. An example of low containment and permeability is great books discussion materials used by advanced groups in their own way. When administrators seek cooperation with an unfamiliar type of continuing education agency, alertness to characteristics associated with boundary maintenance may make it easier to establish satisfactory interagency relationships.

There are, of course, stronger impediments to local cooperation among agencies, such as traditions of separate competition for funds and participants. For local agencies that receive public funds, categorical funding from state and federal sources can encourage independent entrepreneurial approaches. If local administrators prefer greater cooperation, one way to promote it is to suggest that funds be allocated to encourage and reward collaboration. This would probably require a persuasive rationale that such an arrangement would reduce total costs, improve access, increase participation, and strengthen impact. Other ways to encourage collaboration among providers include continuing education councils for formal agencies, learning exchanges for informal providers, and educational brokering services to assist individual adults to use provider services in coordinated ways (Peters and Associates, 1980, Chap. 4.)

Perhaps the best basis for sustained and mutually beneficial collaboration is a symbiotic relationship based on shared purposes, complementary contributions, and shared benefits. This is illustrated by continuing medical education in community hospitals provided by schools of medicine, in which the schools receive referrals to the teaching hospital of patients with specialized health problems upon which the school depends for teaching and research.

Larger Society

Some leadership strategies pertain to generalized relationships with the larger society such as trends related to general economic conditions, financial support, extent of competition, or enrollment trends. One result of such trends can be changes within the agency which have implications for leadership strategies most likely to be effective under the circumstances. The most widespread and attractive trend for continuing education agencies has been growth. Although a boon to most aspects of administration, rapid growth can reduce agreement on agency values and procedures. Strategies for coping with rapid expansion include work teams, decentralization of responsibilities, increase of formal communication, standardization of procedures, and centralization of fiscal control. Stable organizations tend to be resistant to change which makes them vulnerable to crises such as administrative succession. Strategies for administering stable agencies include use of traditional procedures, democratic decision making, gradual problem solving, open and accurate records, and clear procedures for designation of successors.

Declining organizations are usually most difficult to administer, in part because of multiple problems that cannot all be solved internally. Morale tends to decline as commitments and expectations are not met. Strategies for administering declining agencies include reducing nonessential parts and reallocating resources to essential parts and mobilizing internal reformers to support necessary reorganization and to search for new activities that may reverse the decline (Caplow, 1976). It is ironic that continuing education agencies may be reduced by parent organizations experiencing decline, in part because they fail to appreciate the contribution that continuing education could make to new goals and activities to help reverse the decline.

Policy, Authority, and Influence

For some major decisions, internal and external considerations come together. These tend to be policy decisions. Effective directors, as the heads of any organizations, try to make a few careful strategic policy decisions instead of many quick problem-solving choices. A sound strategic decision should benefit from a broad perspective but should be as simple and pertinent to the working level as possible (Drucker, 1966). Following are important features of effective policy making:
1. Conclude that a problem was generic and required a policy decision.
2. Define the boundary conditions or specifications that a solution to the problem should meet.
3. Identify the best solution for the specifications before attention to adaptations to make the decision acceptable.
4. Build into the decision the actions to implement it.
5. Include feedback to test the soundness of the decision against the actual course of events.
6. Have the courage to proceed with a sound but difficult decision.

Leadership strategies depend in part on agency size. In small agencies authority relationships and decision-making procedures among staff members resemble those in an egalitarian family. By contrast, large agencies with many departments handling specialized functions that require coordination call for a formal authority structure and decision making.

As Walker (1979) noted, administrators of educational institutions in which others have substantial power and who emphasize their status, authority, purpose, and their will to make hard decisions and enforce rules tend to be ineffective administrators. Their overly moralistic view of their role encourages them to view decision making as including remaking and coercing people, defending territories, and punishing the wicked. Dissent and opposition to administrative policies are discouraged. This is not an explicit strategy but an implicit cosmology.

In contrast, Walker (1979) characterizes higher education institutions as having many power centers, only one of which is the central administration. In his democratic political view of decision making, the dynamic organization reflects outside pressures and legitimate internal constituencies with differing interests. As a result, conflict and even opposition to administrative decisions are inevitable. In such a setting, criticism is accepted and even encouraged sometimes because progress results from dialectical change in which differing opinions collide.

In this democratic political approach to administration, part of an agency director's role would be to preside over a decision-making process that would make conflict productive for the organization. This is especially important when there is competition for scarce resources. Such an approach calls for attention to organizational structures and climates, people's feelings and power, and especially trust. In this pragmatic problem-solving process, decision making is not a discrete activity but part of a chain that includes consensus building, bargaining, and compromise where major decisions are affected by those that precede them and affect those that follow.

As Cohen and March (1974) also emphasize, effective use of this administrative strategy calls for a sense of direction, persuasion, and perseverance to use procedures that encourage the expansion of human potential in a problem-solving process aimed at achieving desirable results. Especially in larger agencies and parent organizations, it will take a balanced and somewhat dispersed team to provide the wisdom and diplomacy needed to identify the main and most timely issues to pursue, to build consensus, and to persist in the pursuit of results. Walker (1979) characterized this administrative style as pushy diplomacy, in which wisdom and a sense of direction are combined with persistence and diplomacy in which goals are set and problems solved with the simplest workable means by people close to the problems and opportunities. As Griffiths (1959) emphasized decades ago, the heart of leadership is decision making about the decision-making process.

Summary and Conclusions

Decisions regarding external relations can take all the leadership an administrator can muster. Many such decisions include attention to priorities or collaboration. Policy makers, administrators, and others from the parent organization, other providers, and the larger society are typically involved. Under these circumstances, the continuing education administrator's formal authority yields a relatively small amount of power to make decisions regarding external relations, in contrast with the other power centers with which he or she deals. This is especially so when the continuing education function is decentralized within the parent organization.

In these circumstances, effective administrators understand the needs and expectations of other people associated with the decision-making process, leaders and followers alike. This is both more important and more difficult when the other people are associated with other agencies in which their traditions regarding purposes, styles, and boundary maintenance, if not understood, can make collaboration difficult. Effective collaboration usually reflects shared purposes, complementary contributions, and satisfactory benefits to all parties. Such empathy is even important within the parent organization, in which the continuing education agency typically has more permeable boundaries than the remainder of the parent organization. This is one of the few advantages of marginality (another is flexibility), because it can make it easier to serve hard-to-reach adults.

Decisions related to the larger society tend to be even more global and diffuse. Events and trends (such as new legislation, loss of appropriations, economic trends, or increased competition from other providers) are influential but it is often not clear whom to engage in the decision-making process. As a result, the administrator reacts to rising costs or declining enrollments.

As a result, decision-making strategies regarding external relations tend to be more global, complex, and varied than most of the internal agency decisions regarding such choices as changes in program, staff, facilities, or the marketing mix. External strategies often entail multiple goals, participants in the decision-making process, and influences. Bargaining and tradeoffs are typical. In this process, the ways in which continuing education administrators acquire and use influence may be as important to the success of leadership strategies as the formal steps in decision making.

The following qualities of leadership suggest desirable administrative styles:

1. Having a sense of direction that helps achieve consensus on desirable outcomes among people with differing values whose cooperation is important to making and implementing a decision.
2. Having expertise regarding decision making and program development that is valued by others associated with the decision-making process.
3. Having a low need for power and a willingness to rely on gentle persuasion and influence.
4. Being flexible and dealing with differences in goals and preferred procedures as occasions for problem solving and administrative creativity.
5. Being aware of the needs and aspirations of oneself, staff, policy makers, and clientele while engaging in decision making that tends to emphasize externals.
6. Being persistent, using pushy diplomacy, and nudging so that parties to decisions often believe it was their own idea and are committed to making the decision work.
7. Recognizing that making sound external decisions is often a team effort in which the specific persons associated with an agency who can be most successful will vary from instance to instance.

Effective administrators influence agency goal setting, but other people in and outside the agency do so as well. Because of these differing values and expectations, effective leadership strategies should emphasize consensus building. And because of their power-poor positions, much of the influence of continuing education administrators reflects the cumulative effect of their persuasiveness and their many small decisions on various aspects of program administration.

Discrepancies between an individual's current decision-making procedures and the concepts and procedures that others have found useful can help an administrator strengthen leadership strategies.

Discrepancy Analysis

Administrative decision making is an unavoidably personal process and can hardly be otherwise, since a continuing education director's access to pertinent information is combined with personal assumptions and values. However, effective decision making, especially in continuing education settings, is also a public process in that other people must be involved. Administrators accomplish their goals with the help of other people, and their involvement in the decision-making process contributes to consensus on desirable objectives and to commitment to help achieve these objectives. Also, participation in the decision-making process can be a valuable vehicle for staff development.

Perhaps the best way to improve decision making is to help those involved recognize discrepancies between the procedures they use and those that other administrators have found helpful. Making decision-making goals, assumptions, and procedures more explicit and public enables administrators to recognize discrepancies between current and other, more desirable procedures.

This volume has reviewed examples from practice and concepts from the professional literature to indicate some of the resources available to continuing education administrators interested in strengthening their decision-making abilities. The concepts and examples were organized around major decisional areas such as priority setting, resource allocation, marketing, program coordination, staffing, and external relations. This concluding chapter suggests ways to compare pertinent concepts with current decision-making practices in order to identify desired improvements.

Decision making is a complex process in which an administrator's values and expertise are combined with situational expectations and circumstances. Administrators who discover how others take conceptual, belief, technical, human, and other organizational aspects of administration into account can appreciate the advantages of making their own decision making more public. Directors who discover that some of their most important decisions are about the decision-making process are also likely to discover how much they can learn from others about decision-making strategies (Andrew and Moir, 1970; Bennis and others, 1976; Newell and Simon, 1972; Richman and Farmer, 1974). This view contrasts with that of administrators who emphasize themselves as the sole decision makers who exercise their unique knowledge of the situation and the goals they pursue.

Priority setting can include some of the most complex and value-laden choices. If priority setting entailed selecting the most desirable objective, the process would be relatively simple. Instead, at best it usually entails seeking agreement on objectives in the face of conflicting goals and influences. Some of the most difficult decisions entail choices among several desirable alternatives. The dilemma of people who confront conflicting expectations and values is one of society's most enduring and perplexing themes. Administrators who understand this are likely to use strategies that include agency staff, resource persons, policy makers from the parent organization, and potential participants from the service area in the decision-making process. Administrators who discover that decision making is not just a rational process but one that entails bargaining and compromises can give more attention to the human and political aspects of the process.

Resource acquisition, allocation, and accounting require attention to finance and other resources. Consideration of such resources is central to much administrative decision making. Mastery of concepts and procedures regarding finance and accounting is essential to making sound finance-related decisions. Administrators without such understanding are slaves to the process instead of masters. However, resources are means to ends, and the entire decision-making process about finance-related issues requires attention to value judgments and local circumstances. Even selection and interpretation of financial data depend on purpose and setting. Administrators who discover this realize that many financial problems have largely programmatic solutions.

Marketing concepts apply to strengthening mutually beneficial exchanges between an agency and various publics including potential participants, resource persons, and policy makers. The concept of a fair exchange contributes to development of decision strategies, such as the idea of a marketing mix, that place specific decisions about recruiting participants into the framework of a general marketing approach. Administrators who discover a rationale that ties together isolated decisions related to marketing can use either a general rationale or a specific decision tree to avoid overlooking important alternatives and to decide who should be included in the process. Effective administrators are able to use major concepts and procedures flexibly.

Program development activities that occur throughout a large agency are quite varied and together can be very complex for an administrator to supervise. Inexperienced administrators who have difficulty distinguishing important from unimportant features of a complex situation try to avoid becoming overwhelmed by oversimplifying. In contrast, effective administrators recognize strategic factors that can be influenced and that make a difference. These factors constitute the intermediate models that guide their predictions of probable relationships. For example, mastery of program development procedures (such as for needs assessment, objective setting, or evaluation) enable a supervisor to help inexperienced but promising resource persons to increase their effectiveness. Also administrators who understand the great importance of interpersonal relations (such as working with planning committees) can contribute to both program effectiveness and staff development and, in addition, can increase their flexibility and responsiveness as they work with those who help adults learn. Understanding the interconnectedness of components of program development can also help administrators facilitate the flow of decisions and involve others in the process.

Staffing decisions are especially important because it is the resource persons, administrators, and support staff members who make most of the other decisions on which so much of program quality depends. Effective supervision includes attention to both productivity and satisfaction. Conflict and differing expectations can lower staff satisfaction. Effective administrators seek to emphasize integrity and trust so that differences lead to creative tension instead of divisiveness. Administrators who discover such generalizations related to staffing explore ways in which they can become more effective talent managers, utilize multiple incentives, and use procedures for staff development and organizational change that are appropriate for their situation.

External relations with the parent organization and with other providers and groups in the service area involve decentralized decision making, which calls for leadership at its best. Leaders with centralized power can rely on the authority of their position and the ability to invoke sanctions to influence the others' actions. Most continuing education administrators are in power-poor positions and must use decision-making strategies that depend heavily on persuasion to win and maintain cooperation. Administrators who discover this seek to understand the political and bureaucratic dynamics in their situation, to use diplomacy to deal with conflicting values and expectations, and to use bargaining and compromise to achieve agreement on objectives and cooperation for achieving those objectives. They realize that internally, as well as externally, effective administration is more like teaching than like ordering.

Effective decision-making strategies typically entail aspects of several of the foregoing decisional areas. Choices that relate only to finances or only to staffing tend to be relatively straightforward. Because most major decisions include attention to priorities, resources, staff, and program development, effective administrators orchestrate specialized contributions to an ongoing decision-making process. Administrators who discover this increase their attention to policy making and decision making about the decision-making process. When the problem to be solved is well defined, some fairly routine decision making strategies can be used (Bell and Coplans, 1976; Brown,

Kahr, and Peterson, 1974; Davis, 1973; Richards and Greenlaw, 1972). However, when administrators confront unfamiliar and ill-defined problems, procedures for problem solving and decision making tend to change accordingly (Duncan, 1973; Johnson, 1972; Mack, 1971; Miller, 1970; Vinacke, 1974; Vroom and Yetton, 1973).

Concepts relevant to decision making can be helpful in several ways. Reading about, or discussing with peers, other ways to view a decisional issue and procedures to resolve it can broaden administrators' perspectives and help them recognize discrepancies between their leadership approach and approaches that may be more effective. Contact with organized knowledge can also enable administrators to analyze those discrepancies and consider alternative strategies. Findings from research and conclusions from the experience of others can be woven into the strategies themselves and used to critique them as part of an ongoing process of renewal. As with program development and decisional strategies, effective ways to strengthen the process of decision making tend to be developmental and evolutionary. However, as important as knowledge is for leadership, to benefit decision making, knowledge must be combined with the courage to act.

References

Allison, G. T. *Essence of Decision.* Boston: Little, Brown, 1971.
Anderson, R. E., and Kasl, E. S. *Costs and Financing of Adult Education and Training.* Lexington, Mass.: Lexington Books (forthcoming).
Andrew, G. M., and Moir, R. E. *Information-Decision Systems in Education.* Itasca, Ill.: Peacock, 1970.
Argyris, C., and Schön, D. A. *Theory in Practice: Increasing Professional Effectiveness.* San Francisco: Jossey-Bass, 1974.
Aslanian, B., and Brickell, H. M. *Americans in Transition: Life Changes as Reasons for Adult Learning.* New York: College Entrance Examination Board, 1980.
Barrows, H. S., and Tamblyn, R. M. *Problem Based Learning.* New York: Springer, 1980.
Beckhard, R. *Organization Development: Strategies and Models.* Reading, Mass.: Addison-Wesley, 1969.
Bell, R. I., and Coplans, J. *Decisions, Decisions: Game Theory and You.* New York: Norton, 1976.
Bennis, W. G. *Organization Development: Its Nature, Origins, and Prospects.* Reading, Mass.: Addison-Wesley, 1969.
Bennis, W. G., Benne, K. D., Chin, R., and Corey, D. E. *The Planning of Change.* New York: Holt, Rinehart and Winston, 1976.
Blake, R. R., and Mouton, J. S. *The Managerial Grid.* Houston, Texas: Gulf Publishing Company, 1964.
Bock, L. K. *Teaching Adults in Continuing Education.* Urbana: University of Illinois Office of Continuing Education and Public Service, 1979.
Brown, M. A., and Copeland, H. G. (Eds.). *New Directions for Continuing Education: Attracting Able Instructors of Adults,* no. 4. San Francisco: Jossey-Bass, 1979.
Brown, R. V., Kahr, A. S., and Peterson, C. *Decision Analysis.* New York: Holt, Rinehart and Winston, 1974.
Buskey, J. H. (Ed.). *New Directions for Continuing Education: Attracting Funds for Continuing Education,* no. 12. San Francisco: Jossey-Bass, 1981.

Chamberlain, M. N. (Ed.). *New Directions for Continuing Education: Providing Continuing Education by Media and Technology,* no. 5. San Francisco: Jossey-Bass, 1980.
Caplow, T. *How to Run Any Organization.* Hinsdale, Ill.: Dryden Press, 1976.
Clark, B. R. *Adult Education in Transition.* Berkeley: University of California Press, 1956.
Cohen, M. D., and March, J. G. *Leadership and Ambiguity.* New York: McGraw-Hill, 1974.
Collins, B. E., and Guetzkow, H. *A Social Psychology of Group Processes for Decision Making.* New York: Wiley, 1964.
Daigneault, G. H. *Decision Making in the University Evening College.* Chicago: Center for the Study of Liberal Education for Adults, 1963.
Darkenwald, G. G. "Innovation in Adult Education: An Organizational Analysis." *Adult Education,* 1977, *27* (3), 156-172.
Darkenwald, G., and Larson, G. A. (Eds.). *New Directions for Continuing Education: Reaching Hard-to-Reach Adults,* no. 8. San Francisco: Jossey-Bass, 1980.
Davidson, S., and Weil, R. (Eds.). *Handbook of Cost Accounting.* New York: McGraw-Hill, 1978.
Davis, G. A. *Psychology of Problem Solving: Theory and Practice.* New York: Basic Books, 1973.
Delbecq, A. L., Van de Ven, A. H., and Gustafson, D. H. *Group Techniques for Program Planning.* Glenview, Ill.: Scott, Foresman, 1975.
Deppe, D. A. "The Adult Educator: Marginal Man and Boundary Definer." *Adult Leadership,* 1969, *18* (4), 119-120, 129, 130.
Drucker, P. F. *The Effective Executive.* New York: Harper and Row, 1966.
Duncan, W. J. *Decision Making and Social Issues.* Hinsdale, Ill.: Dryden Press, 1973.
Eble, K. E. *The Art of Administration.* San Francisco: Jossey-Bass, 1978.
Fiedler, F. E. *A Theory of Leadership Effectiveness.* New York: McGraw-Hill, 1967.
Foley, R. P., and Smilansky, J. *Teaching Techniques.* New York: McGraw-Hill, 1980.
Gagné, R. M., and Briggs, L. J. *Principles of Instructional Design.* New York: Holt, Rinehart and Winston, 1974.
Griffiths, D. E. *Administrative Theory.* New York: Appleton-Century-Crofts, 1959.
Hackman, J. R., Lawler, E. E., and Porter, L. W. (Eds.). *Perspectives on Behavior in Organizations.* New York: McGraw-Hill, 1977.
Hentschke, G. C. *Management Operations in Education.* Berkeley, Calif.: McCutchan, 1975.
Herzberg, F. *Work and the Nature of Man.* New York: World, 1966.
Hodgson, R. S. *Direct Mail and Mail Order Handbook.* (2nd ed.) Chicago: Dartnell, 1974.
Houle, C. O. *The Design of Education.* San Francisco: Jossey-Bass, 1972.
Johnson, C. F. "Bicycles, Tricycles and Continuing Medical Education." *Journal of the Tennessee Medical Association,* May 1978, pp. 345-351.
Johnson, D. M. *A Systematic Introduction to the Psychology of Thinking.* New York: Harper & Row, 1972.
Katz, D., and Kahn, R. L. *The Social Psychology of Organizations.* (Rev. ed.) New York: Wiley, 1978.
Knowles, M. S. *Self-Directed Learning.* New York: Association Press, 1975.
Knowles, M. S. *The Modern Practice of Adult Education.* (Rev. ed.) New York: Association Press, 1980.
Knox, A. B. *Social System Analysis of the Adult Education Agency.* New York: Center for Adult Education, Teachers College, Columbia University, 1967.
Knox, A. B. "Life-Long Self-Directed Education." In R. J. Blakely (Ed.), *Fostering the Growing Need to Learn.* Rockville, Md.: Division of Regional Medical Programs, Bureau of Health Resources Development, 1974.
Knox, A. B. "New Realities in the Administration of Continuing Higher Education." *The NUEA Spectator,* 1975, *39* (22), 6-9.
Knox, A. B. *Adult Development and Learning: A Handbook on Individual Growth and Competence in the Adult Years for Education and the Helping Professions.* San Francisco: Jossey-Bass, 1977.

Knox, A. B. *New Directions for Continuing Education: Enhancing Proficiencies of Continuing Educators*, no. 1. San Francisco: Jossey-Bass, 1979.
Knox, A. B. (Ed.). *New Directions for Continuing Education: Teaching Adults Effectively*, no. 6. San Francisco: Jossey-Bass, 1980a.
Knox, A. B. *University Continuing Professional Education.* Urbana: University of Illinois Office for the Study of Continuing Professional Education, 1980b.
Knox, A. B., and Associates. *Developing, Administering, and Evaluating Adult Education.* San Francisco: Jossey-Bass, 1980.
Kotler, P. *Marketing for Non-Profit Organizations.* Englewood Cliffs, N.J.: Prentice-Hall, 1975.
Kreitlow, B. W., and Associates. *Examining Controversies in Adult Education.* San Francisco: Jossey-Bass, 1981.
Lawrence, P. R., and Lorsch, J. W. *Developing Organizations: Diagnosis and Action.* Reading, Mass: Addison-Wesley, 1969.
Levinson, H. *The Exceptional Executive.* Cambridge, Mass.: Harvard University Press, 1968.
Lindquist, J. *Strategies for Change.* Berkeley, Calif.: Pacific Soundings, 1978.
Lusterman, S. *Education in Industry.* New York: Conference Board, 1977.
Mack, R. P. *Planning on Uncertainty.* New York: Wiley-Interservice, 1971.
Mann, D. *Policy Decision-Making in Education.* New York: Teachers College Press, Columbia University, 1975.
March, J. "Education and the Pursuit of Optimism." *Texas Tech Journal of Education*, 1975, *1*, 16.
Maslow, A. S. *Motivation and Personality.* New York: Harper & Row, 1954.
Maslow, A. S. *Eupsychian Management.* Homewood, Ill.: Richard D. Irwin, 1965.
Mezirow, F., Darkenwald, G., and Knox, A. B. *Last Gamble on Education.* Washington, D.C.: Adult Education Association, 1975.
Miller, J. R. *Professional Decision Making.* New York: Praeger, 1970.
Mintzberg, H. *The Nature of Managerial Work.* New York: Harper & Row, 1973.
NJCSEE (National Joint Committee on Standards for Educational Evaluation). *Standards for Evaluation of Education Programs, Projects and Materials.* New York: McGraw-Hill, 1981.
Newell, A., and Simon, H. A. *Human Problem Solving.* Englewood Cliffs, N.J.: Prentice-Hall, 1972.
Pennington, F. (Ed.). *New Directions for Continuing Education: Assessing Educational Needs of Adults*, no. 7. San Francisco: Jossey-Bass, 1980.
Pennington, F., and Green, J. "Comparative Analysis of Program Development Processes in Six Professions." *Adult Education*, 1976, *27* (1), 13-23.
Pepper, S. *The Sources of Value.* Berkeley: University of California Press, 1958.
Peters, J. M., and Associates. *Building an Effective Adult Education Enterprise.* San Francisco: Jossey-Bass, 1980.
Prince, G. M. *The Practice of Creativity.* New York: Harper & Row, 1970.
Richards, M. D., and Greenlaw, P. S. *Management: Decisions and Behavior.* (Rev. ed.) Homewood, Ill.: R. D. Irwin, 1972.
Richman, B. M., and Farmer, R. N. *Leadership, Goals and Power in Higher Education: A Contingency and Open-Systems Approach to Effective Management.* San Francisco: Jossey-Bass, 1974.
Schein, E. H. *Career Dynamics: Matching Individual and Organizational Needs.* Reading, Mass.: Addison-Wesley, 1978.
Schneider, B. *Staffing Organizations.* Pacific Palisades, Calif.: Goodyear, 1976.
Sergiovanni, T. J., and Carver, F. D. *The New School Executive.* New York: Harper & Row, 1980.

Spear, G. E. (Ed.). *Adult Education Staff Development: Selected Issues, Alternatives, and Implications.* Kansas City: University of Missouri, Center for Resource Development in Adult Education, 1976.

Steinmetz, L. L. *Managing the Marginal and Unsatisfactory Performance.* Reading, Mass.: Addison-Wesley, 1969.

Suter, E., and Green, J. S. "Continuing Education of Health Professionals: Proposal for a Definition of Quality." *Journal of Medical Education,* 1981, *56,* 687–707.

Varney, G. H. *An Organization Development Approach to Management Development.* Reading, Mass.: Addison-Wesley, 1976.

Vinacke, W. E. *The Psychology of Thinking.* (2nd ed.) New York: McGraw-Hill, 1974.

Votruba, J. C. (Ed.) *New Directions for Continuing Education: Strengthening Internal Support for Continuing Education,* no. 9. San Francisco: Jossey-Bass, 1981.

Vroom, V. H., and Yetton, P. W. *Leadership and Decision Making.* Pittsburgh, Penn.: University of Pittsburgh Press, 1973.

Walker, D. E. *The Effective Administrator.* San Francisco: Jossey-Bass, 1979.

Wirt, F. M. *The Polity of the School: New Research in Educational Politics.* Lexington, Mass.: Lexington Books, D. C. Heath and Co., 1975.

Index

A

Action, in priority setting, 13
Administration: assumptions in, 13; centralized and decentralized, 90-91, 92-93
Administrative costs, in cost accounting, 26, 27, 28, 30, 31, 32
Administrator: decision-making role of, 4-7; effectiveness of, influences on, 63-65; situational influences on, 62-64, 65; time management by, 62; value assumptions of, 14
Adult basic education, and hard-to-reach adults, 12, 13, 15
Allison, G. T., 13, 15, 106
Anderson, R. E., 24-25, 26, 28, 29, 32, 33, 106
Andrew, G. M., 104, 106
Argyris, C., 11, 106
Aslanian, B., 42, 106
AT&T, employee education costs of, 29
Authority: and external relations, 90, 99-100; sources of, 90

B

Barrows, H. S., 53, 106
Beckhard, R., 57, 106
Beder, H. W., 21
Beliefs, in priority setting, 13
Bell, R. I., 52, 105, 106
Benne, K. D., 106
Bennis, W. G., 57, 104, 106
Blake, R. R., 63, 76, 106
Bock, L. K., 56, 75, 106
Boundary maintenance, in interagency relations, 97-98
Brickell, H. M., 42, 106
Briggs, L. J., 53, 107
Brown, M. A., 72, 75, 106
Brown, R. V., 52, 105-106
Burlingame, M., 65n
Buskey, J. H., 23, 106

C

Caplow, T., 59, 70, 76, 99, 107
Carver, F. D., 13, 14, 77, 90, 108
Centralization of administration, 90-91, 92-93
Chamberlain, M. N., 61, 107
Chin, R., 106
Clark, B. R., 33, 107
Cohen, M. D., 60, 100, 107
Collins, B. E., 7, 107
Committees. *See* Planning committees
Community college, examples at: of learning center establishment, 54-55; of mailings from, 45; of program transferred to, 95-97; of registration process, 48-50; and shadow college, 17-18; of staff termination, 68-69
Community organizations, cost accounting for, 30-32
Continuing education: for enhanced proficiency, 14-15; settings for, 5
Coombs, F. D., 65n
Coordination, of programs, 53-66
Copeland, H. G., 72, 75, 106
Coplans, J., 52, 105, 106
Corey, D. E., 106
Corporation, and leadership roles, example of, 91, 93-94
Cost accounting: accounting concepts in, 25; administrative costs in, 26, 27, 28, 30, 31, 32; analysis of, 24-34; for community organizations, 30-32; for employer education, 29-30; for higher education, 27-29; implications of variations in, 33-34; income in, 26-27, 31, 32; indirect costs in, 26, 27, 28, 32; instructional salaries in, 26, 27-28, 30, 31, 32; for professional associations, 32; for proprietary schools, 26-27; for public schools, 25-26; and value judgments, 32; and volunteers, 31-32
Cost objects, concept of, 25

111

Cost recovery: for credit and noncredit activities, 28-29; extent of, 21-22
Costs, levels of, 25
Course evaluation, situational influences on, 62-63

D

Dahl, D. A., 23
Daigneault, G. H., 4, 73, 107
Darkenwald, G. G., 4, 12, 15, 42, 56, 61, 75, 80, 107, 108
Davidson, S., 24, 107
Davis, G. A., 106, 107
Decision makers, characteristics of, 6
Decision making: as action, 13; administration role in, 4-7; advantages of explicitness in, 1, 5, 6-7, 103; analysis of, 3-9; aspects of, 2, 9; considerations in, 6; cost accounting implications for, 33-34; and discrepancy analysis, 103-106; and experience of others, 5, 106; on external degree program, example of, 7-8; and external relations, 85-102; on faculty appointment, example of, 3-4; on marketing, 37-52; and priority setting, 11-18; process of, 8; in program coordination, 53-66; on program development and clientele, 7-9; on resources, 19-35; on staffing, 67-83
Decision trees, and marketing, 50-52
Delbecq, A. L., 41, 107
Deppe, D. A., 59, 107
Development: action steps in, 74-75; career, priority setting in, 12; employee, and priority setting, 16-17; human resource, and marketing, 38; of staff, 73-75
Direct mail: copy for, 46, 47-48; elements of, 46; examples of decisions on, 45; handbook for, 46-50; and inquiries, 50; lists for, 46, 47; for promotion, 45-46; and registration of students, 48-50; uses of, 46-47
Discrepancy analysis, by leaders, 103-106
Drucker, P. F., 14, 50, 62, 99, 107
Duncan, W. J., 106, 107

E

Eble, K. E., 14, 57, 107
Education, finance related to, 20-21

External degree program, decision-making process for, 7-8
External relations: analysis of, 85-102; and authority and influence, 90, 99-100; and centralization and decentralization, 90-91, 92-93; conclusions on, 100-102; as cooperative or competitive, 97-98; and discrepancy analysis, 105; interagency, 95-98; with larger society, 98-99; and leadership roles, 91, 93-95; and policy, 99-100; and priorities, 86-90

F

Faculty appointment, decision-making process for, 3-4
Farmer, R. N., 104, 108
Fee setting, influences on, 21-22
Fiedler, F. E., 63, 65, 107
Finance, education related to, 20-21
Financial transformation, cycle of, 23-24
Foley, R. P., 53, 107

G

Gagné, R. M., 53, 107
Green, J., 56, 108
Green, J. S., 57, 109
Greenlaw, P. S., 23, 106, 108
Griffiths, D. E., 100, 107
Guetzkow, H., 7, 107
Gustafson, D. H., 41, 107

H

Hackman, J. R., 59, 77, 107
Hard-to-reach adults: and adult basic education, 12, 13, 15; and marketing, 41-42
Hentschke, G. C., 23, 107
Herzberg, F., 77, 107
Higher education, cost accounting for, 27-29. *See also* Community college; University
Hodgson, R. S., 46-47, 50, 107
Houle, C. O., 56, 75, 107

I

Income, in cost accounting, 26-27, 31, 32

Indirect costs, in cost accounting, 26, 27, 28, 32
Inquiries: responses to, 5-6; suggestions for, 50
Instructional salaries, in cost accounting, 26, 27-28, 30, 31, 32

J

Johnson, C. F., 57, 107
Johnson, D. M., 106, 107

K

Kahn, R. L., 85, 97, 107
Kahr, A. S., 52, 105-106
Kasl, E. S., 24-25, 26, 28, 29, 32, 33, 106
Katz, D., 85, 97, 107
Knowledge, in priority setting, 13
Knowles, M. S., 56, 57, 75, 107
Knox, A. B., 5, 15, 21, 23, 39, 42, 44, 54, 56, 57, 59, 60, 64, 72, 75, 80, 85, 107-108
Kotler, P., 39, 55, 108
Kreitlow, B. W., 21, 108

L

Larson, G. A., 12, 15, 42, 56, 61, 75, 107
Lawler, E. E., 59, 77, 107
Lawrence, P. R., 63, 108
Leadership: and authority relationships, 99-100; dealing with feelings about, 94-95; and organizational dynamics, 94; qualities of, 101; roles in, 91, 93-95. *See also* Decision making
Learning center, decision making for establishment of, 54-55
Levinson, H., 77, 94, 108
Lindquist, J., 18, 61, 75, 80, 108
Lorsch, J. W., 63, 108
Lusterman, S., 29, 108

M

Mack, R. P., 106, 108
Mail. *See* Direct mail
Mann, D., 13, 108
March, J., 13, 108
March, J. G., 60, 100, 107

Marketing: analysis of, 37-52; audit for, 40-41; communication channels for, 42-43; concepts in, 37-43; conclusions on, 52; contributions to, encouraging, 38-39; and decision to participate, 42; decision tree for, 50-52; and discrepancy analysis, 104; and hard-to-reach adults, 41-42; and human resource development, 38; informal, 41; mix in, 42; participation in, encouraging, 41-42; promotional techniques for, 43-46; and responsiveness, 39-40
Maslow, A. S., 13, 77, 108
Mezirow, J., 80, 108
Miller, J. R., 52, 106, 108
Mintzberg, H., 60-61, 62, 108
Moir, R. E., 104, 106
Mouton, J. S., 63, 76, 106
Museum: evolving priorities at, example of, 86-88; fee setting at, 22

N

National Endowment for the Arts, 86
National Joint Committee on Standards for Educational Evaluation (NJCSEE), 56, 108
Newell, A., 104, 108
Nowlen, P. M., 54

O

Orientation: features of, 73-74; means for, 56-57
Outcomes: levels of, 14-15; in marketing, 38; in priority setting, 11-12
Outreach, reorganization of, 80-81

P

Participant learning hours (PLH), cost per, 26, 27, 28, 30, 31, 32, 33
Pennington, F., 56, 75, 108
Pepper, S., 6, 108
Peters, J. M., 98, 108
Peterson, C., 52, 105-106
Planning committees: decisions by, 57-58; influences on, 58-59; for program coordination, 57-59
Porter, L. W., 59, 77, 107
Prince, G. M., 57, 108

Priority setting: action, knowledge, beliefs, and values in, 13; analysis of, 11–18; in career development, 12; choices and outcomes in, 11–12; and competing expectations, 13–14; concepts about, 11–13; and discrepancy analysis, 104; evolution in, example of, 86–88; examples of, 15–18; and external relations, 86–90; influences on, 13–15; and levels of outcome, 14–15; strategies and tactics in, 12–13

Professional association: cost accounting for, 32; priorities of, 88–89

Programs: analysis of coordination of, 53–66; conclusions on, 64, 66; development of, and clientele for, 7–9; and discrepancy analysis, 104–105; for orientation of resource persons, 56–57; origins of, 54–56; planning committees for, 57–59; situational influences on, 62–64, 65; steps in starting, 55–56; supervision of, 59–62; transfer of, example of decisions on, 95–97

Promotional techniques: direct mail as, 45–46; for marketing, 43–46; personal contact as, 44–45; publicity as, 43–44

Proprietary schools, cost accounting for, 26–27

Public schools, cost accounting for, 25–26

Publicity, for promotion, 43–44

R

Registration, changing process of, 48–50

Reorganization: and agency as social system, 80; concepts in, 79–80; of staff, example of, 78–80

Resource persons: identifying, 72–73; orientation of, 56–57

Resources: acquisition and allocation of, 19–24; analysis of, 19–35; and cost accounting, 24–34; and cost recovery, 21–22; and discrepancy analysis, 104; and financial transformation, 23–24; finance and education related to, 20–21; generalizations on, 34–35; sources of, 22–23; technical and value components related to, 24

Responsiveness, marketing and, 39–40

Richards, M. D., 23, 106, 108

Richman, B. M., 104, 108

S

Schein, E. H., 16, 57, 75, 108
Schneider, B., 71, 108
Schön, D. A., 11, 106
Sergiovanni, T. J., 13, 14, 65n, 77, 90, 108
Simon, H. A., 104, 108
Smilansky, J., 53, 107
Spear, G. E., 73, 109
Staff: analysis of, 67–83; conclusions on, 82–83; conflict in, 70; on contract basis, example of, 71; development of, 73–75; and discrepancy analysis, 105; full- and part-time, 72; interpersonal relations of, 69–70; needs of, and motivation to grow, 77; reorganization of, 78–82; selection of, 71–73; supervision of, 75–78; and termination, 67–71
Steinmetz, L. L., 59, 109
Strategies, in priority setting, 12–13
Sulkin, H. A., 21
Supervision: concepts of, 76; decisional roles in, 61–62; indirect, guidelines for, 76; informational roles in, 60–61; interpersonal roles in, 60; and motivation to grow, 77–78; of programs, 59–62; of staff, 75–78; as teaching, 77
Suter, E., 57, 109

T

Tactics, in priority setting, 12–13
Tamblyn, R. M., 53, 106
Termination, of staff, 67–71
Thurston, P. W., 65n
Time, administrative management of, 62

U

University: and federal funds, priority setting and, 15–16; outreach reorganization at, 80–81; responsiveness in marketing at, 39–40

V

Values, in priority setting, 13
Van de Ven, A. H., 41, 107
Varney, G. H., 57, 109
Vinacke, W. E., 106, 109

Volunteers, and cost accounting, 31-32
Votruba, J. C., 18, 61, 64, 73, 85, 109
Vroom, V. H., 106, 109

W

Walker, D. E., 99-100, 109
Weil, R., 24, 107

Wirt, F. M., 13, 109
Workshops and conferences, cost containment for, 20-21

Y

Yetton, P. W., 106, 109

WITHDRAWN
St. Scholastica Library
Duluth, Minnesota 55811